eMAGIC LOGIC
Tips and Tricks
Len Sasso

PC Publishing

PC Publishing
Export House
130 Vale Road
Tonbridge
Kent TN9 1SP
UK

Tel + 44 (0) 1732 770893
Fax + 44 (0) 1732 770268
email info@pc-publishing.com
web site http://www.pc-publishing.com

First published 2003

© PC Publishing

ISBN 1 870775 856

British Library Cataloguing in Publication Data
A catalogue record for this book is available from the British Library

Cover design by Michelle Raki

Printed and bound in Great Britain by Biddles, Guildford

Preface

Logic is an extremely powerful and flexible digital audio workstation. A lot of time has been devoted to making Logic both logical and user friendly, but there's no avoiding the fact that it can take a while to learn your way around. This Tips and Tricks guide is not intended to teach you Logic from the ground up, nor to cover all its many features. It is intended to give you a quick tour of Logic's major features as well as point out as many shortcuts and time saving tricks as possible.

If you're new to Logic, the main flow of text will give you an overview of how Logic works, how to use its unique user interface, and where to find what you need for various aspects of music making. If you know your way around Logic, the main text may refresh your memory on some of the details, but you'll find the tips and notes most useful. For you, the best approach is to scan the sub-headings for topics of interest, dipping in and out of the book as the need and inclination arises.

Throughout the book you'll find boxes labelled *Quick Tip* and *Info*, which contain short tips and feature descriptions. Longer tips and more detailed descriptions are contained in the main text and are usually organized under their own headings. Tips with multiple steps use bullets to indicate the steps.

As Logic has evolved, different ways of naming things have been adopted so that now there is some confusion of terms in the Logic community. In this book, I have adopted the following conventions. Containers for data are always referred to as Regions, whether the data is audio or MIDI. (Elsewhere you may find containers of MIDI data called Sequences.) When I want to distinguish the two I write MIDI Regions and Audio Regions. When I simply write Region, the statement applies to both types. Finally, the word 'object' is reserved for Logic's Environment objects.

One of Logic's most important features for gaining speed and managing the work flow is its extensive set of user-definable key commands. At present there are close to 900 available key commands and more are added with each new version of Logic. Throughout the book, I have indicated key commands (*KC*), their default assignments, and corresponding menu entries (*M*) for the processes discussed. Appendix 2 contains a complete list of available key commands.

This book would not have been possible without the input of hundreds of Logic users over the past five years. I owe a special dept to members of the Logic Users Group. Many of the ideas here sprang from the questions as well as the answers posted on the Users Group list. I also thank my many friends in the Logic community for the constant interchange of ideas and techniques. Appendix 3 contains references to useful links in the Logic community as well as other publications about Logic.

Dedication

To Caia for constant support and especially for putting up with yet another book.

Contents

Setting up Logic

L ogic gives you the freedom to configure it to suit your needs and wishes. Unfortunately, some of that configuring needs to be done at the outset, possibly before you understand what's involved. In version 6 (OS X only), Logic has simplified the task by providing the Logic Setup Assistant (LSA), which will walk you though a series of questions, configuring Logic based on your answers. That's a good way to start, but you will eventually want to make adjustments and understand what's going on under the hood. That's what this chapter is about.

Global versus Local settings

Global settings apply to all your Logic songs. They include your MIDI and Audio setup and drivers, display and operational preferences, control surface settings, and Key Commands. You can change any of the Global settings at any time and the changes will apply to all songs, old and new.

Info

In OS X the Preferences file is named info.emagic.logic and is found in the **User** » **Library** » **Preferences** directory. In OS 9 it is named Logic Preferences and found in the **System** » **Preferences folder**.

Local settings belong to and are saved with individual songs. They include recording, MIDI, synchronization, and score settings as well as Screensets, Transform sets, Hyper Edit sets, and the Environment. You can import most local settings from other songs. Logic maintains default local settings, which it uses whenever you create a new song.

The Logic Setup Assistant (LSA)

If you're using Logic in OS X, the Logic Setup Assistant can walk you through a series of dialogs and set up Logic's Preferences and default song according to your answers. If you are running Logic for the first time or have moved or deleted Logic's preferences file, LSA will start automatically when you launch Logic. You can also launch LSA directly from the Desktop. Here is a brief rundown of the LSA screen sequence including where you can make similar settings within Logic. If you're not using LSA, these steps still might be useful to know:

Quick tip

You can create your own default settings by saving a song with the name *Autoload* in the same directory as the Logic application. See below for suggestions on setting up your own Autoload song.

Quick tip

If you already have Preferences and Key Commands set up, it is a good idea to move them to a new location before running the LSA. That way you can get back to your old setup if need be.

1

- Detect Devices: this is an optional scan for your MIDI and audio hardware devices. You can add and remove devices manually later. Logic doesn't have a built-in auto detection scheme, but you can enable specific drivers in the Preference sections: *Audio Drivers* and *Communications*.
- Audio: if you opted to detect devices, choose the device you wish to use for Logic's audio input and output from those shown here. You can change this later in Logic's *Audio Driver* Preferences.
- Mixer Setup: this screen creates five types of Audio objects in Logic's Environment: tracks, busses, instruments, inputs, and outputs. Set the numbers according to your audio interface specifications and your audio i/o needs or choose from one of the supplied presets. These choices also determine how Logic's default Mixer and Arrange window will be laid out (hence the name). Within Logic, Audio objects are created in the Environment and Arrange track assignments are made in the Arrange window.
- Audio Inputs: this setting determines how your audio tracks will be set up for live audio recording. The settings here can be changed for individual Audio objects at any time. Audio inputs can be assigned to Audio objects in the Environment, the Mixer, or the Arrange window.
- Key Commands: you can choose from six sets of default key commands or you can leave your present set unchanged if you have already set one up. If you're a ProTools or PowerKeys user, you'll probably want to choose the corresponding set and if you're mainly working on a laptop, you'll probably want to choose the US or German Powerbook setup. The key command references *KC* and *•KC* throughout this book refer to the US Pro Keyboard set. Key commands can be defined in the Key Commands window. You can also initialize all key commands there.
- Screensets: nine default Screensets, which can be recalled with the number keys 1 through 9, are created. If you have a multiple monitor setup, the LSA will take advantage of that. Screensets are part of each individual Logic song. You can make your own default song, called Autoload, to create your own default Screensets for starting new songs.
- MIDI Devices: a list of detected MIDI devices is presented here. Any devices you leave on the list will be available. If you want some devices to not be used by Logic, delete them. MIDI Devices can be enabled using the Audio MIDI Setup utility on OS X, and in the Communications Preferences of Logic on other platforms.

After you accept the LSA choices, Logic's Preferences and default song will be set up. If you already have an Autoload song, Logic will use that instead of the default song when it starts up and when you create a new song.

The Environment

There are a few things you need to know about the Environment to get started. (We'll take a deeper look into this fascinating and sometimes daunting aspect of Logic in Chapter 4.)

KC   Open Environment window «CO 8»

Quick tip

To open the Logic default song when you also have an Autoload song, select **File » Open** while holding the Option key.

Info

KC = Key Command.

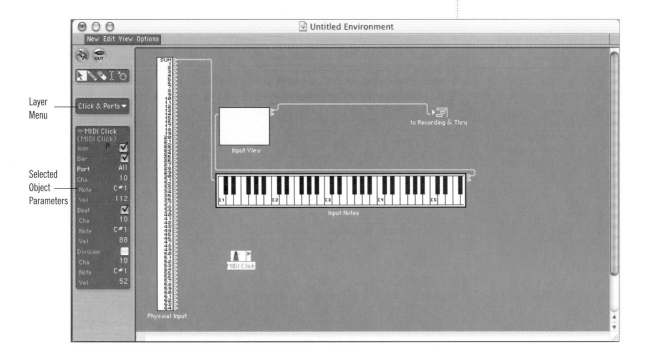

Layer Menu

Selected Object Parameters

The Environment window is organized in Layers for more convenient viewing and cabling. You can place any kind of object on any Layer, freely move objects between Layers, and even draw cables from one Layer to another.

Figure 1.01
Logic's Environment window. Logic's audio and MIDI signal flow is managed here by creating objects for MIDI and audio input and output, and in the case of MIDI, drawing cables between them.

Info

The Environment is saved with the song, and each song can have a different Environment. Typically you will start with the Environment in your Autoload song or Logic's default song and make additions or changes in individual songs as needed.

The three important Layers in Logic's default song Environment are Clicks & Ports, MIDI Instr, and Audio.

The Clicks & Ports Layer manages the transfer of data from external devices (i.e. your MIDI controllers) to Logic's MIDI sequencer (i.e. Arrange window tracks). By default it contains a Physical Input object (incoming MIDI data), a to Recording & Thru object (the pipeline to Arrange window tracks), a Keyboard object for creating as well as viewing notes, and a Monitor object for viewing all MIDI data in list form. That setup is handy for seeing what's going on and for creating MIDI notes without an external MIDI device.

The MIDI Instr. Layer contains a 16-channel Multi-Instrument and a Mapped Instrument. The Multi-Instrument is an example of how to route MIDI to a multi-channel MIDI device and the Mapped Instrument is an example of the special handling of drums on MIDI channel 10. This is one area in which you will need to expand and modify the Environment to suite your MIDI studio. If you have an extensive MIDI rig, you will probably use several Layers to accomplish that. See Chapter 4 for more details.

Info

If you delete the Physical Input and to Recording and Thru objects, Logic will route all incoming MIDI data directly to the track selected in the Arrange window, and the Keyboard object's output will also be routed there.

The Audio Layer contains Audio objects for audio playback (from audio tracks in the Arrange window), audio inputs (from your sound card), audio outputs (to your sound card), audio instrument plug-ins, effects bus returns, and other special audio routing (e.g. ReWire buses).

Preferences

Each of the settings on Logic's 11 Preference pages is covered in detail in Logic Help and the Logic manual. Here, by Preference page, are some tips for the more important settings.

Communications
On platforms other than OS X, this is where you enable possible MIDI interface ports. In OS X that is handled by the Audio MIDI Setup utility.

Global
Use this window to set up various aspects of Logic's behaviour. Of particular interest:

* Choosing which editor window opens when you double-click a MIDI Region in the Arrange window – choose the editor you're most comfortable using.
* Deciding whether to leave windows for different songs open at the same time. Leaving them open allows you to click to change songs and to drag items between songs, but also results in more cluttered screens.
* Deciding whether to automatically empty the Trash when a song is saved. Logic's Trash is an often overlooked emergency backup for deleted MIDI Regions, but leaving it full causes your songs to grow larger. Since the Trash is not automatically emptied unless this is enabled, you should enable it or manually empty the trash regularly.

    KC   Empty Trash
    KC   Open Trash

* Whether to use Logic's Auto Backup function, which will keep a backup of the latest versions of your song. Up to 100 versions can be archived, but off, 1, or 3 seem like reasonable choices.

Display
This window controls various Logic display parameters. *The Display Middle C as C3* checkbox should be checked for consistency with most MIDI devices. When unchecked, Logic will display Middle C as C4. (Here, Middle C refers to MIDI note number 60 rather than a particular pitch.)

The Sort Instrument Menu By... checkboxes and the *Use Hierarchical Menus* checkbox control the organization of the Instrument menu that pops-up when you click-hold on the name of an Arrange window track. If you have a large number of MIDI and Audio objects, you should definitely use hierarchical menus. Beyond that, the sorting preferences are a matter of personal taste.

Reset messages

Logic now handles MIDI message resets dynamically using its Smart Reset algorithm. Therefore, all boxes should be unchecked.

Audio

The critical settings here are *Sample accurate automation*, and *Freeze File Format*. Sample accurate automation increases CPU load. Unless you are really limited, it should be on for Volume, Pan, and Sends. If you have lots of CPU power and use plug-in automation, turn it on for that, too.

The Freeze File Format should be the default 32-bit unless you need to import Freeze Files into Logic or another application after-the-fact. You might need to do that when moving a song with frozen tracks from OS 9 to OS X for example, if some of your plug-ins have not made the switch. In that case choose 24-bit, because Logic won't import 32-bit files.

Audio driver

Obviously, pick the driver for the sound card(s) you want Logic to address.

The I/O Buffer Size will affect audio instrument plug-in latency. Lower numbers mean lower latency and more CPU drain. The Rewire behaviour affects the latency when playing instruments linked to Logic using ReWire. Live mode results in lower latency and higher CPU drain.

The Universal Track Mode setting controls whether Logic uses one or two Audio objects for stereo input and playback. When checked, Logic uses a single audio object for stereo. That is more convenient and uses fewer Audio objects, but prevents you from separately busing the channels of a stereo signal. If you don't need to do that, leave it checked.

Compatibility

Unless you know you need to do otherwise, leave the defaults: New Phase Control Timer Model, Smooth Cycle Algorithm turned on, Global tempo Correction turned off.

Song settings

Unlike Logic's Preferences, which are saved separately and apply globally, Logic's Song settings are saved with individual songs and can be different for each song. There are two Song Settings windows: a Synchronizations window for setting up various MIDI synchronization protocols and a Song Settings window with 13 sub-windows. Both windows are opened from the File menu. As with the Preferences, the individual settings are well documented in the Logic manual and Logic Help and I'll only discuss a few of them here.

Metronome settings

Logic can now provide a metronome click in two ways: by MIDI output and using the special Audio Instrument, Klopfgeist, which by default is installed in Audio Instrument object 64. In case of MIDI you can specify the MIDI channel, note number, velocity for bar, beat, and division clicks, and the desired MIDI output port. For Klopfgeist you can specify note number, velocity, tone, level, and audio output.

Figure 1.02
The Metronome Settings window allows you to set up Logic's metronome to play either an external MIDI device or the built-in audio instrument, Klopfgeist.

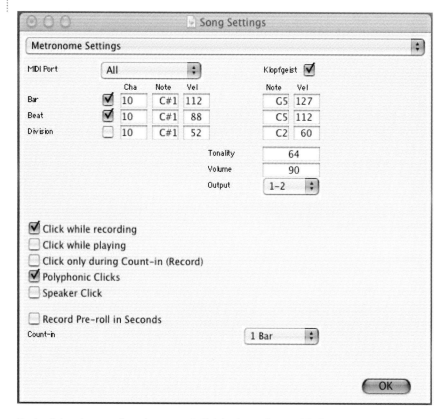

Each click category (bar, beat, and division) can be enabled separately and clicks can be restricted to recording, playback, or recording pre-roll.

Both the MIDI output and Klopfgeist plug-in are accessible from the Environment as well. The MIDI output is handled by the *MIDI Metronome Click* object, which by default is on the Clicks & Ports Layer. Klopfgeist is automatically inserted in Audio Instrument object #64, which by default is placed on the Audio Layer.

Recording options

Use this section to control how Logic handles cycle recording (multiple takes), whether recordings are merged or kept in separate Regions, whether MIDI controller data is 'thinned' to save MIDI bandwidth on playback, and whether to record tempo changes.

MIDI options

Use this section to filter out incoming MIDI data that you don't want to record or pass through to the output. Any MIDI message class can be disabled, but typically you should leave everything enabled except possibly SysEx and Poly-Pressure. SysEx can take up a lot of bandwidth, and unless you're recording MIDI-device program dumps, you probably don't need to deal with it. Likewise Poly-Pressure takes a lot of bandwidth and many MIDI devices don't respond to it. You would likely disable it if your MIDI keyboard sends it, but none of your MIDI devices responds to it.

You can select one Environment object for which incoming MIDI data is not passed through to its output when it is assigned to an Arrange track. The default is a pseudo-object appropriately named 'No Output'. If you have a MIDI device for which you can't turn MIDI Thru off (some older synths have that problem) you might want to select the Environment Instrument you use for it instead.

Chase events

When you start playback in the middle of a song, you may want the MIDI settings that occur before the start point to be sent, thereby putting your MIDI devices in the state they would have been had you started playback from the beginning. You can also choose whether you want to chase events when you jump back to the beginning of a cycle. Of course, deciding to chase events has the potential to greatly increase the data flow when you start playback or cycle-jump. Unless you encounter MIDI bandwidth problems, it's a good idea to enable chase for everything except MIDI notes and to enable it for cycle jumps.

Old songs

Before Logic's Track Based Automation, which uses special internal messages rather than MIDI, all plug-in automation was done with MIDI controller messages. That type of automation, called Region Based Automation (RBA), is still available, and is useful, for example, when plug-ins have their own MIDI controller mapping for automation.

Logic offers two schemes for RBA using MIDI controller messages: send all controller messages directly to Instrument plug-ins or divide the controllers among the various plug-in slots. In the latter case, Logic overrides the plug-ins MIDI assignments with its own scheme. You can choose between those methods with the *Software Instruments Use* menu on the Old Song page. You'll probably want to set it to *MIDI Controllers as standard MIDI controls* so that you can use the full spectrum of MIDI controller messages for your software instruments.

Creating your Autoload song

Although Logic's default song is a good starting point, you will undoubtedly develop your own favourite Screensets, Environment layout, and other Song Settings as you work with Logic. To make those the starting point for new songs, save a song with your favorite settings using the name Autoload.

Here are some tips for creating an effective Autoload song:

- Use a minimal set of tracks in the Arrange window consisting of several of the kinds of tracks you use most. For example, include two audio playback tracks, an audio output track, and a few MIDI tracks for the synths you use most. That will easily fit on most displays and leave room to open an editor window. Convenient key commands allow you to easily insert more tracks as you need them.

KC   Create Track *«SH Return»*
KC   Create Track with next Instrument *«SH CT Return»*

Quick tip

To avoid overwriting your Autoload song, designate it as stationery in the Finder's Get Info dialog. Then each time you create a new song in Logic, it will be named Untitled, and you will be prompted to rename it the first time you save.

Info

Any song that is saved as stationery will load as an untitled song.

- Keep a full complement of Audio and MIDI Instrument objects in the Environment, but limit other Environment processes to those you use often. You can easily import special-purpose Environment processes that you use rarely, if you set them up properly in the first place (see Chapter 4 for details).
- Create single-digit Screensets for each editor window using the same number as opens the editor window itself. For example, if «CO 6» opens the Matrix editor, devote Screenset 6 to a Matrix editor Screenset.

Quick tip

An effective strategy until you settle on a specific design is to strip all the data (including tempo changes and referenced audio files) from your latest song and save it as your Autoload. As you use Logic more, you will establish work habits that automatically get integrated into your Autoload song.

Loading, saving, importing and exporting

Logic songs have their own, proprietary format which is sometimes identified by the extension '.lso'. When you save a Logic song, it will always be saved in that format.

Logic can also import and export files in a number of common formats including standard MIDI files (SMF), Open Media Framework (OMF), and Open Track List (OpenTL). Options for doing so are found on the File menu under Import and Export.

Quick tip

On some occasions, Logic may not recognize Logic songs saved on another platform (Windows versus MacOS). In that case you can use the Import function on Logic's File menu to open the songs. If you then save them, they will open normally in the future.

Info

Files created by versions 5 and later of Logic are not compatible with earlier versions of Logic. But all later versions of Logic can export files in Logic 4.8 format. Unsupported features such as Track Based Automation (see Chapter 6) are not exported in that format.

Windows, screensets and key commands

P robably no single factor is more important in becoming a Logic power user than learning the many shortcuts for viewing and manipulating objects in Logic's various windows. Each window affords a unique view into the data of your song, and each has shortcuts tailored to its specific view. In fact, the next four chapters, the bulk of this book, are devoted to Logic's windows.

The Arrange window (Chapter 3) provides a timeline overview of your song. The Environment window (Chapter 4) manages Logic's entire signal flow. The Mixer window (Chapter 5) provides onscreen control of audio and MIDI mixing functions. Four MIDI editor windows (Chapter 6) provide different views for entering and editing MIDI data. The Audio window (Chapter 8) is for managing all your audio files. The Sample Editor window (Chapter 11) provides numerous digital signal processing (DSP) functions. The Project Manager (Chapter 12) allows you to organize all your Logic songs and all the data files to which they refer.

Screensets are window arrangements on your computer display. 90 screensets are readily available, and a few tricks will reveal some more should you ever need them.

Almost anything you can do with the mouse in Logic, you can also do with some combination of keys on your computer keyboard. In fact, there are a number of things you can do only with key commands. Logic gives you free rein to assign its key commands to your computer keyboard in any way you find convenient. Spending some time learning and assigning key commands will speed up your Logic sessions enormously.

KC   Open Key Commands *«OP K»*

Working with windows

Figure 2.01
Most of Logic's windows feature two-dimensional scrolling, two modes of linking with other open windows, synchronization to the current playback position, and recallable snapshots for size and scroll position. The Arrange window is shown here.

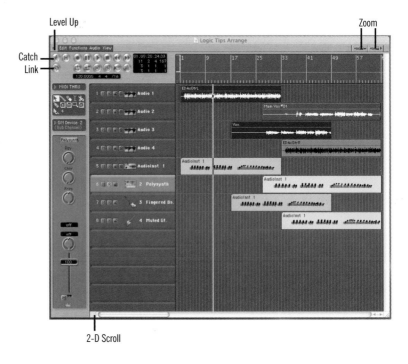

Opening and closing windows

Logic has a key command for opening each of its windows. By default these are assigned to the number keys with the Command key modifier *(«CO #»)*.

If you use the Command+Option modifier combination the window will open as a floating window *(«CO OP #»)*.

Navigating levels

Many of Logic's windows support multiple levels of viewing. In the Arrange window that means moving in and out of Folders, which can even be nested. In the Event and HyperEdit windows, it means both moving in and out of Folders and moving in and out of MIDI data Regions. In the Matrix and Score windows, it means moving from viewing the data within a single MIDI Region to simultaneously viewing the data within several Regions.

- For windows that support viewing the MIDI data in multiple Regions, double-click an event in one of the Regions to view only the data in that Region.

- For windows that support viewing Region frames or the MIDI data within them, double-click on a Region frame to view the data inside.
- In the Arrange window, double-click a Folder to move inside; double-click a MIDI Region to view its data in the preferred editor (which you set in the Global Preferences); and double-click an audio Region to open the Sample Editor.
- In any window you can double-click an empty area or the Level-Up box in the upper-left corner to move up one level.

Linking and synchronizing windows

Most of Logic's windows can be synchronized in two ways: they can automatically scroll horizontally during playback to keep the current playback position in view, and they can automatically change the Region they are displaying in coordination with other open windows. Of course, you can toggle those features on and off, on a case-by-case basis.

The Catch button with the running-man icon turns automatic scrolling on (blue) and off (grey). The Link button with the chain-link icon controls synchronization of different windows. It has three states: off (grey), Link (pink), Contents Link (yellow). As far as is possible, a window in Link mode will display the same data as is displayed in the top (active) window. As far as is possible, a window in Content Link mode will display the data inside any object that is selected in the top window. Of course, Arrange windows cannot display the contents of MIDI or audio Regions (i.e. MIDI or audio data) and the Event editor is the only MIDI editor that can display Regions and Folders as well as their contents. So linking is not effective in all situations.

When Catch and Content Link are both turned on in a MIDI editor window, the window's contents will change as playback moves into different Regions on the same Track. That is not the case with the Sample Editor window, however.

KC   Catch Clock Position «V»
KC   Link Window (Same Level)

Zooming and snapshots

There are several ways to change the magnification (zoom) of Logic's windows. The two buttons with the telescope icons on the top-right border of the window affect vertical zoom (down arrow) and horizontal zoom (right arrow), respectively. Clicking the wide end of the telescope increases the magnification (less data displayed), while clicking the small end decreases it. Each window also has its own three-zoom memory.

KC   Save as Zoom # (1-3)
KC   Recall Zoom # (1-3)

When you hold the Control key and press the mouse button, the cursor becomes a magnifying glass and the window will automatically zoom to fit any area that you select by dragging.

To make matters even more convenient, Logic maintains a navigation history containing the last 30 magnification settings and scroll positions. The following operations automatically cause the current settings to be stored in the navigation history:

- Using the magnifying glass to change magnification.
- Using any of the magnification key commands except the Navigate Forward and Navigate Backward commands.

KC   Zoom to fit Selection vertically and horizontally, store Navigation Snapshot «Z»
KC   Zoom to fit Selection horizontally, store Navigation Snapshot
KC   Zoom to fit Locators, store Navigation Snapshot
KC   Store Navigation Snapshot
KC   Navigation: Back «SH Z»
KC   Navigation: Forward

Scrolling and scrubbing

In any of Logic's time-based windows (Arrange, Matrix, Score in linear mode, Event, and Hyper Editor), you can use key commands to move forward and backward in one or eight measure steps. The key commands just move the SPL – Catch (see above) must be enabled for the window to scroll along with the SPL.

- KC   Forward
- KC   Rewind
- KC   Fast Forward «SH ,»
- KC   Fast Rewind «SH .»

In addition to using forward/rewind key commands, you can use the Arrange window's Solo tool (see Chapter 3) to scrub back and forth. The scrubbing must be done in the Arrange window, but if another window's Catch is enabled, its display will follow along.

Working with screensets

There are 90 screensets that can be recalled by number using the number keys at the top of the computer keyboard or on the numeric keypad. All digits except zero can be used to recall Screensets by number. To recall Screensets with two-digit numbers, hold the Control key while entering the number.

You can use Meta events in MIDI Regions and in the Environment to access screensets with numbers containing zero as well as those numbered 100 and above. See Chapter 4 on the Environment for details.

Number keys on your computer keyboard can also be assigned to other key commands, however that could cause you to lose keyboard access to screensets using those numbers. To avoid that, leave one of the keys for each number unassigned by using the Key Command window's Learn Separate Key option (see below).

As mentioned, unless a screenset is locked, any changes you make become part of the current screenset.

KC   Lock/Unlock Current Screenset *«SH L»*

Screensets are saved separately for each song and it's a good idea to set up your autoload song with screenset layouts that you intend to use frequently.

M   File » Song Settings » Import Settings

Working with key commands

The good news is that Logic has 875 key commands. The bad news is that Logic has 875 key commands. Furthermore, the number goes up with each new version. Although with four modifier keys (Shift, Command, Control, and Option) there are enough key combinations to cover them all, remembering them is another matter. In short, you'll need to be choosy to make the best use of Logic's key commands.

If you use Logic Setup Assistant (see Chapter 1) to configure Logic, you've already chosen one of Logic's default key command configurations: ProTools, PowerKeys, or Logic 6 Default.

Info

The PowerKeys setup has been developed over years of extensive consultation with Logic professionals. You can order a set of stick-on labels for those commands at the PowerKeys Web site (see Appendix 3).

References to available key commands are sprinkled liberally throughout this book. Key commands with menu or tool equivalents are indicated by *KC*. Actions that can be accomplished only with key commands are indicated by •*KC*. When there is Logic 6 Default key command, it is shown within wedges *«»*. Modifier keys are abbreviated as: *SH* for Shift, *CO* for Command, *OP* for Option, and *CT* for Control.

The Key Commands window

Key command assignments are made in the Key Commands window, which can be opened from the Logic menu or with a key command.

M   Logic » Preferences » Key Commands...
KC   Open Key Commands... *«OP K»*

Key command assignments (both computer keyboard and MIDI) can be made using menus in the Info box at the top left or by using the three Learn buttons beneath it.

Info

When a Screenset is locked, there is a bullet to the left of the word 'Window' in the Mac Menu Bar.

Info

M = menu item.

Quick tip

You can import all of a song's Screensets into another song using the File menu.

Quick Tip

Not all key commands apply in all Logic windows. When a key command has different meanings in different windows, its function is determined by the top window.

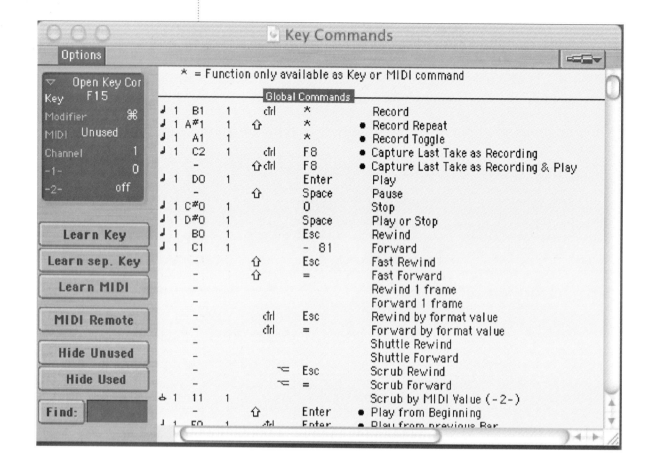

Figure 2.02
The Key Commands window allows you to assign any computer keyboard key with any combination of modifiers (Shift, Command, Option, and Control) to over 875 actions. You can also assign MIDI remote commands.

Using MIDI remote commands

MIDI remote commands work a little differently than computer keyboard commands—they can be turned on or off. That allows you to assign MIDI notes to key commands and still use MIDI for playing the notes. MIDI Remote can be turned on using the MIDI Remote button in the Key Commands window. You can also assign a MIDI remote key-command to it, and that command will always be active.

KC Toggle MIDI Remote (always MIDI remotable).

Cataloguing your key commands

The Options menu at the top of the Key Commands window, has a selection to copy the key commands in text format to the Macintosh Clipboard. From there they can be pasted into a text document or spreadsheet for printing and organizing.

Quick tip

The Learn Separate Key (Learn sep. Key) button allows you to assign a computer keyboard key according to its location on the computer keyboard instead of its keycap. That allows you to assign separate commands to the number keys along the top and those on the numeric keypad, for example.

Quick tip

Copying to the Clipboard reflects the current view state of the Key Commands window. Click Hide Used or Hide Unused to copy only those key commands. Use the Find function to copy only key commands containing a specific reference.

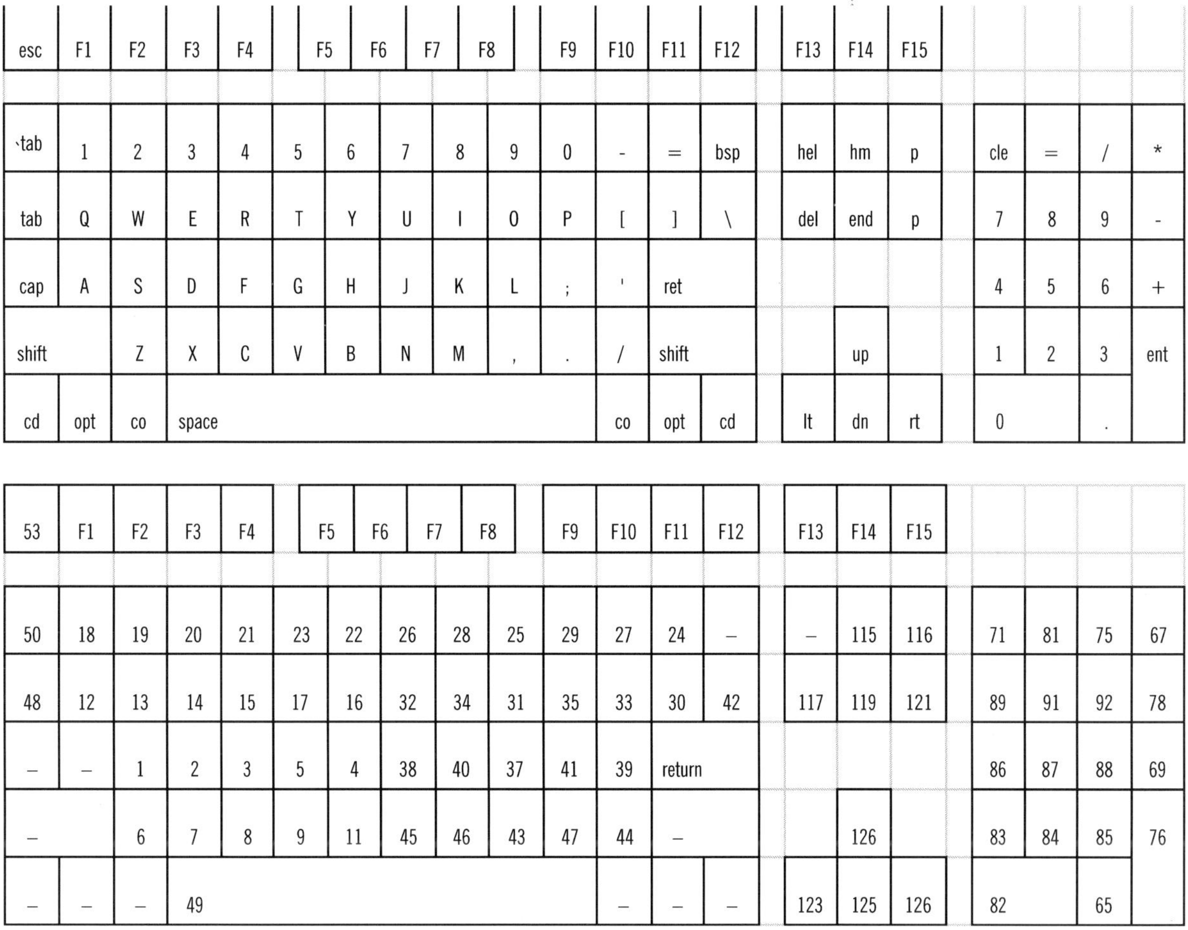

esc	F1	F2	F3	F4	F5	F6	F7	F8	F9	F10	F11	F12	F13	F14	F15					
˙tab	1	2	3	4	5	6	7	8	9	0	-	=	bsp	hel	hm	p	cle	=	/	*
tab	Q	W	E	R	T	Y	U	I	O	P	[	]	\	del	end	p	7	8	9	-
cap	A	S	D	F	G	H	J	K	L	;	'	ret					4	5	6	+
shift		Z	X	C	V	B	N	M	,	.	/	shift		up			1	2	3	ent
cd	opt	co	space						co	opt	cd		lt	dn	rt		0		.	

53	F1	F2	F3	F4	F5	F6	F7	F8	F9	F10	F11	F12	F13	F14	F15					
50	18	19	20	21	23	22	26	28	25	29	27	24	–	–	115	116	71	81	75	67
48	12	13	14	15	17	16	32	34	31	35	33	30	42	117	119	121	89	91	92	78
–	–	1	2	3	5	4	38	40	37	41	39	return					86	87	88	69
–		6	7	8	9	11	45	46	43	47	44	–		126			83	84	85	76
–	–	–	49						–	–	–		123	125	126		82		65	

If you paste the key commands into a spreadsheet program, you will get separate columns for the modifier-key combination, the assigned key, and the command description. Sorting by the assigned-key column provides a useful alternate view of your key commands, and makes it easy to find which keys have been assigned.

Figure 2.03
The numbers indicated for key commands assigned using Learn Separate Key correspond to the standard MacAlly key codes shown here. Illustration courtesy of Hendrik Veenstra.

Quick tip

Before sorting by columns in a spreadsheet, create a new column and place row numbers in its cells. Sorting by the new column will then restore the original order.

Tools of the trade

Each Logic window has its own collection of tools for manipulating objects. Tools such as the Selector tool are available in all windows whereas others like the Solo and Mute tools appear only in windows containing objects that can be soloed or muted. Here is a brief description of each tool's function:

Figure 2.04
Tools available in Logic's windows.

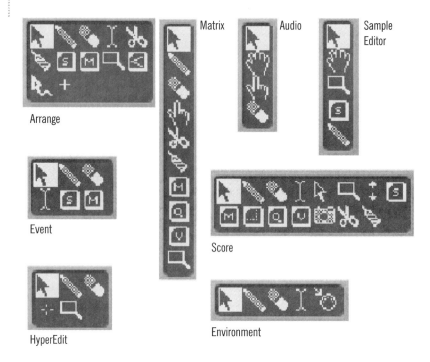

• The Selector tool (arrow icon) is for selecting and moving objects.
• The Pencil tool is for creating objects.
• The Eraser tool is for deleting objects.
• The I-Beam tool is for entering text.
• The Scissors tool is for splitting objects.
• The Glue tool (glue tube icon) is for merging objects.
• The Solo tool (S) is for soloing objects.
• The Mute tool (M) is for muting objects. It can be applied to Regions or individual notes.
• The Wedge tool (<) is for creating fades in the Arrange window.
• The Magnifier tool is for setting the zoom level by click-dragging.
• The Automation tool (crooked arrow icon) is for creating automation curves.
• The Marquee tool (+) is for selecting two-dimensional areas in the Arrange window.
• The MIDI tool (MIDI connector icon) is for assigning Environment objects to Arrange tracks.
• The Camera tool is for taking pictures of sections of the Score window.
• The Finger tool is for changing note lengths in the Matrix window and for changing audio Region lengths in the Audio window.
• The Crosshair tool is for creating contours in the HyperEdit window.
• The Quantize tool is for quantizing notes in the note editors.
• The Velocity tool is for editing note Velocities in the Matrix and Score editors.

KC   Show Tools *«Esc»*
KC   Set Next Tool
KC   Set Previous Tool

Quick tip

The Show Tools command opens the Toolbox at the cursor location so that you can select a tool without moving the mouse very far.

Quick tip

You can set an alternate tool, which will be activated when you hold the Command key, by holding the Command key and clicking on the desired alternate tool.

The Arrange window

The Arrange window is a track and timeline overview of the arrangement of your song. Two types of data containers can appear on Arrange window tracks: Regions and Folders. Regions may contain MIDI or audio data. Folders contain Regions. Each song has only one arrangement, but Folders can be used to organize song sections and to some extent, to hold alternative song arrangements.

Regions

Regions contain data of two types, MIDI and audio. MIDI data can be recorded directly from an external MIDI controller, in which case a Region will automatically be created to contain it, or entered in various ways using Logic's several MIDI editors (see Chapter 8). Non-note MIDI data can even be drawn in directly in the Arrange window using Hyper Draw.

Audio data can also be recorded directly in the Arrange window, in which case an audio file will be created on your hard drive and placed in the song's Audio window. A Region pointing to the full audio file will be placed in the Arrange window at the song position at which it was recorded.

In a confusing but convenient twist, audio Regions can also contain MIDI data. That happens when you Hyper Draw Region Based Automation (see Chapter 6) directly onto an audio Region. The data can be viewed and edited in any of the MIDI editors (see Chapter 8), but there is no separate physical Region containing it. (It can of course, be cut and pasted into a normal MIDI Region if you want to separate it from the audio region.)

Split and merge

Regions of like kind can be freely split and merged, but merging has different consequences for MIDI and audio Regions. Splitting simply produces separate Regions of the same type. You can split with the Scissors tool, or using various key commands.

KC   Split Objects by Song Position
M   Arrange » Functions » Split/Demix » Split Objects by Song Position
KC   Split Objects by rounded Song Position
KC   Split Objects by Locators
M   Arrange » Functions » Split/Demix » Split Objects by Locators

Regions can be merged using the Glue tool or various key commands. The newly formed Region extends from the beginning of the leftmost to the end of the right-most Region being merged. For MIDI Regions, the 'per Tracks' option results in separate Regions on each track that contains a selected Region. Otherwise select-ed MIDI Regions are merged into a single Region, as is done with the Glue tool. (The per tracks option has no effect when merging audio Regions.)

KC   Merge Objects/Digital Mixdown «-30» (]-Separate Key)
M   Arrange » Functions » Merge » Objects
KC   Merge Objects per Tracks «SH +»
M   Arrange » Functions » Merge » Objects per Tracks

Info

For audio Regions, the merge function produces a new audio file containing the audio data within each of the selected Regions. But Logic is smart enough to know if a new file is not needed – for example, when two adjacent Regions from the same audio file are being merged.

Stretch and shrink

You can move either end of a Region without affecting the data within. In the case of audio, you are limited by the ends of the audio file to which the Region refers. For MIDI Regions you can't move the left end to the right of the first MIDI event in the Region. (You can move the right end to the left of MIDI events in the Region, and the events will then not be played back.) To move the edge of a Region, place the cursor over the edge to be moved and when the icon turns to an index finger, click and drag.

You can also stretch and shrink Regions, though this action has different mean-ings and methods for audio and MIDI Regions. To stretch or shrink a MIDI Region, move the cursor to the right end of the Region and when the icon turns to an index finger, click and drag while holding the option key. You will be asked to confirm the stretching. The effect will be to move the MIDI events in time while preserving their relative positions (meaning later events will be moved farther than earlier ones).

Stretching and shrinking audio Regions is done from the Functions menu or with a key command. There are two options: stretching or shrinking to the nearest bar-line and to the length between the Locators. In either case the Region remains anchored to its original time position. The process results in a new audio file that has been processed by one of Logic's Time and Pitch Machine algorithms – you can choose which one from the Functions menu.

KC   Adjust Object Length to Locators «CT T»
KC   Adjust Object Length to nearest bar «SH CT T»
M   Arrange » Functions » Objects » Adjust Object Length to Locators
M   Arrange » Functions » Objects » Adjust Object Length to nearest bar
M   Arrange » Functions » Objects » Time Machine Algorithm

Quick tip

Splitting by rounded Song Position is useful for cutting up a Region on the fly while Logic is playing—you can be a bit late on the trigger and still get splits at the barlines.

Quick tip

The Scissors tool scrubs a lot like the Solo tool (see below). Click-dragging with the Scissors tool plays the audio or MIDI at the location of the tool and drag-speed controls playback speed. But, unlike the Solo tool, the playback does not continue when you stop dragging. The actual split isn't made until you release the mouse button. Audio scrubbing works only if your audio hardware supports it

Info

Merging audio files takes into account both pan and volume settings, but does not process any effects inserts. For that you need to use the Bounce function (see Chapter 9).

Quick tip

For more complex time shifting, for example to match tempo, double-click the Region to open it in the Sample Editor, then use the Time and Pitch Machine from the Factory menu (see Chapter 10 for details).

Alias and loop

There are two ways to repeat a Region without creating a copy: use an Alias or turn on Loops. An Alias is a pointer to the original Region and can be placed anywhere on the same or a different track. Looping causes a Region to be repeated on the same track until it encounters another Region. You can create an Alias of an audio or MIDI Region by Shift-Option-Dragging the Region to a new location.

Info

Any changes to the original of an Aliased Region also affect the Alias. You can double-click the original or the Alias to make changes.

Quick tip

You can also control the duration of looping by packing the looped Region into its own Folder and setting the Folder length to the desired Loop duration. That process does not work for loops of audio Regions, however – they may continue playing beyond the end of the Folder.

Quick tip

Looping for audio Regions can cause synchronization problems if the Region is not exactly cut to a barline. That often happens when fine tuning audio Regions with Search Zero Crossings enabled (which is the preferred method). Using Aliases is a safer alternative.

Quick tip

When you want to modify some occurrences of a looped Region, first turn Loops to Aliases then turn those Aliases you want to modify to real copies. That will leave you with far fewer copies (and therefore less data) than converting all the loops to real copies. If you want the changes to propagate from where they occur, delete the Aliases that are left, and turn looping on for all the real copies that are left.

You turn on looping for a Region in its Region Parameter Box (see below). To end the looping, create an empty Region at the desired end location.

M   Arrange » Functions » Alias » Make
KC Make Alias
M   Arrange » Functions » Alias » Turn to Real Copy
KC Turn Alias to Real Copy
M   Arrange » Functions » Alias » Reassign
KC Reassign Alias «SH CO R»
M   Arrange » Functions » Alias » Select Original
KC Find Original of Alias «CO R»
M   Arrange » Functions » Alias » Select All Aliases of Object
KC Select All Aliases of Object «SH A»
M   Arrange » Functions » Alias » Select All Orphan Aliases
M   Arrange » Functions » Alias » Delete All Orphan Aliases
M   Arrange » Functions » Sequence Parameter » Turn Loops to Real Copies
KC Turn Loops to Real Copies «K»
M   Arrange » Functions » Sequence Parameter » Turn Loops to Aliases
KC Turn Loops to Aliases

Folders

As mentioned, Folders have many uses. For example, they can:

- Hold song sections.
- Hold all Regions of a particular type – for example, all drum parts.
- Hold alternate takes.
- Hold alternate song arrangements (with limitations).

M   Arrange » Functions » Folder » Pack Folder
KC Pack Folder «CO F»
KC Unpack Folder «SH CO F»

Quick tip

When you want to unpack only some items in a Folder, first pack the items you don't want unpacked into a Folder within the Folder. Then unpack the main Folder, and the inner Folder will now contain the items you wanted to remain packed.

Arrangements within Folders are not completely independent, because they all share the same tempo, time-signature, and key-signature changes as well as the same Track Based Automation. In the case of tempo, you can have 10 alternative tempo lists (see Chapter 7), which could be used in conjunction with different Folders.

KC	Select Next Song
KC	Select Previous Song
KC	Select Song #

Info

The select-song key commands can take a while to execute during which time it will look like nothing is happening. Logic is working behind the scenes—be patient.

Navigating Folders

As with all Logic windows (see Chapter 2), you can have more than one Arrange window open in the same screenset and they can have different view settings. That's especially useful when you want to drag Regions into, out of, or between Folders (See Figure 3.01 overleaf).

Quick tip

You can drag a Region in to a Folder in the same Arrange window, but the only way to control its track and time-position is to drag it in to an open Folder in another Arrange window.

Quick tip

To open a second Arrange window showing the contents of a Folder, select the Folder first, then use the Windows menu or Open Arrange window key command.

A Folder is a container, just like any other Region. The difference is that it contains Regions rather than MIDI, or audio data. Folders can be relocated, resized, looped, and aliased just like Regions.

You can create Folders within other Folders, and in that sense, you can think of Folders as levels within an Arrangement. The main Arrange window is the top level. The contents of Folders in the Arrange window are on the second level. The contents of Folders within those Folders are on the third level, etc.

Quick tip

To collect a group of Regions in a Folder, select the Regions and use the menu command **Arrange » Functions » Folder » Pack Folder**. If no Regions are selected, you will get an empty Folder with the same tracks as the Arrange window, but without any Regions in it.

Quick tip

When you want to evolve completely separate arrangements of the same song, save the song under an alternate name. You can have more than one song open at a time, and even drag data between them.

Quick tip

To avoid confusion about who's on top, it's a good idea to open additional Arrange windows as floating windows. Add the Option key to the Key Command or Windows menu selection to do so.

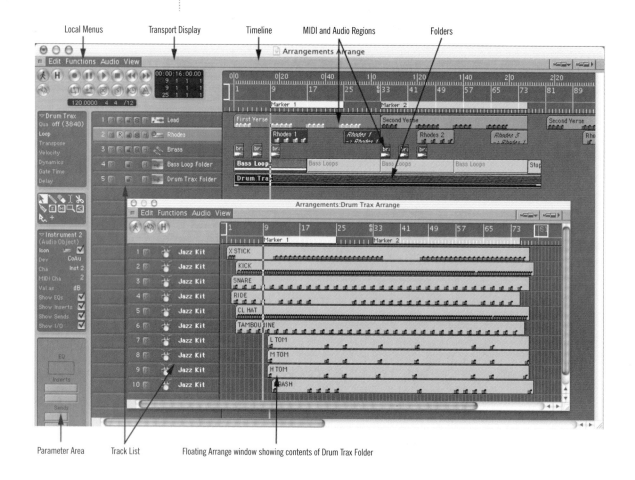

Local Menus   Transport Display   Timeline   MIDI and Audio Regions   Folders

Parameter Area   Track List   Floating Arrange window showing contents of Drum Trax Folder

Figure 3.01
Two Arrange windows, one normal and the other floating. The floating window (inset) shows the contents of the drum tracks Folder.

Quick tip

To move in to a Folder (down one level) and display its contents in the same Arrange window, double-click it. To move out of a Folder (up one level), double-click any empty area in the Folder display or click the double-box at the top-left corner of the Arrange window.

Getting around in the Arrange window

The main section of the Arrange window, where the Regions are arranged, is bordered by four important displays: the Bar Ruler (top), the Transport (top-left), the Track List (mid-left), and the Parameter Area (far left).

KC Hide/Show Parameters *«P»*

The top of the Arrange window, which normally contains the local menu items, becomes an Info display whenever you select a Region. The information updates in real time as you make changes to the Region. From left to right it tells:

• What action is about to take place (move, copy, lengthen, divide, etc.)
• The position of the Region on the Bar Ruler. (For audio Regions this is the position of the anchor, not necessarily the left edge of the Region.)
• The name of the Region.
• The number of the track the Region is on.
• The length of the Region.

The Bar Ruler

Figure 3.02
The Bar Ruler display shows bars and beats, time-signature changes see bar 33), Marker locations (see Marker 1), the cycle or skip area (the shaded section), and an optional SMPTE time display (at the top).

In addition to the bars and beats display, the Bar Ruler displays the current cycle or skip range, Marker positions, time-signature changes, and an optional SMPTE time display.

KC Positions/Bar Ruler in SMPTE units *«U»*

Logic maintains three locators – Left Locator, Right Locator, and Song Position Locator (SPL) – each of which can be set graphically or numerically in the Transport display. The SPL is Logic's current playback position. The Left and Right Locators control the time-range within which Logic's playback will cycle or alternatively, the time-range Logic will skip over during playback. Cycling occurs when the Left Locator is before the Right Locator and skipping occurs when the Right Locator is before the Left Locator (giving new meaning to the terms 'right' and 'left'). Cycling and skipping can be turned off regardless of the Locator positions.

KC Cycle *«/»*
KC Swap Left and Right Locator *«J»*

Info

When the SMPTE time display is turned on, the position and length of the selected Region is shown in the Info display as time rather than as bars and beats.

KC   Move Locators forward by Cycle Length *«SH CO Right Arrow »*
KC   Move Locators backwards by Cycle Length *«SH CO Left Arrow»*

Markers

Markers serve three purposes in Logic:

- They mark time-positions in the Arrange window.
- They hold text notes.
- They delimit song sections.

Markers can be created on the fly as a song plays, they can be created from a selection of Regions, in which case they will take on the Region names, and they can be created by dragging the cycle range downward into the Marker zone of the Bar Ruler. All Marker actions can be accomplished from the global menu or with Key Commands.

M   Options » Marker » ...
KC   Create Marker *«OP CO Up Arrow»*
KC   Delete Marker *«OP CO Down Arrow»*
KC   Open Marker Text ... *«CO T»*
KC   Open Marker List... *«CO L»*

Quick tip

To set the Left and Right Locators graphically, click and drag in the bars and beats portion of the Bar Ruler display. Dragging right creates a cycle, whereas dragging left creates a skip.

Info

Logic maintains a separate pair of locators for punch-in recording. When punch-in recording is activated, the lower half of the shaded portion of the Bar Ruler shows the punch-in locators and the upper half shows the cycle locators. They can be moved independently.

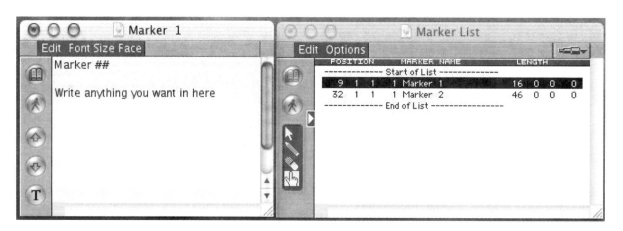

Figure 3.03
The Marker window can display text you've entered (left) or a list of all Markers (right). If Catch mode is turned on the Display will automatically update to show the Marker at the current playback position. The Marker window can be opened as a floating window.

Quick tip

You can use single Key Commands to simultaneously jump to a Marker's position, turn on cycle mode, and set the Left and Right Locators to the Marker's boundaries.

KC   Set Locators by previous Marker & Enable Cycle *«OP CO ,»*
KC   Set Locators by next Marker & Enable Cycle *«OP CO .»*
KC   Goto Marker # *«OP CO F#»*
KC   Open Object Colors *«C»*

The Transport

In addition to controlling record, playback and scrubbing operations, Logic's Transport window and the transport display in the upper-left corner of the Arrange window contain cycle, punch in/out, tempo, time signature, MIDI I/O, and song length information. All those values can be edited numerically or by click-scrolling.

Figure 3.04
The Transport window can be displayed in a number of different formats, chosen from the pop-up menu that opens using the arrow in its lower-right corner. Most of the Transport data will also be displayed in the upper-left corner of the Arrange window if **Arrange » View » Transport** is turned on.

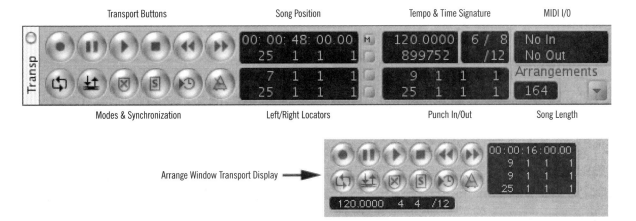

Transport Buttons   Song Position   Tempo & Time Signature   MIDI I/O

Modes & Synchronization   Left/Right Locators   Punch In/Out   Song Length

Arrange Window Transport Display ➡

Here's a brief summary of the Modes & Synchronization buttons (bottom row) from left to right:

- Toggle cycle playback.
- Toggle punch in/out recording.
- Toggle record-replace mode.

- Toggle Solo modes.
- Synchronization toggle and pull-down menu.
- Metronome toggle and pull-down menu.

The Track List

The Arrange window's Track List controls the playback destination of Regions on each track. Playback takes place using various types of Environment object (see Chapter 4) for MIDI and audio data.

There are several ways to assign an Environment object to a track. The simplest is to click-hold on a track in the Track List then select the object from the drop-down Instrument menu that appears. (The format of the Instrument menu can be set in Logic's Display Preferences.) You can also drag objects from the Environment window to the Track List. Finally, the Environment's MIDI tool can be used to assign any clicked object to the currently selected track.

Info

A track must already be created before you can assign it a destination. To create a new track, double-click on an empty portion of the Track List.

KC   Append Track to Track List
KC   Append Track to Track List with next Instrument
KC   Create Track «SH Return»
KC   Create Track with next Instrument «SH Return»
KC   Delete Track
KC   Delete Unused Tracks «OP CO Backspace»

Track List display options

The Track List display is very flexible. You can toggle various display elements on and off using the View menu. In addition you can designate tracks as hidden then use the Hide/Show button (H icon) to the left of the transport section of the Arrange window to toggle the display of all hidden tracks.

KC   Toggle Hide View «H»
KC   Hide Track «CT H»
KC   Unhide all tracks «CT OP H»

Optional Track List display elements include:

- Track numbers and level meters.
- Mute, Record, Protect, and Freeze buttons.

Quick tip

When the Mute button is hidden, you can mute the track by clicking at the far left of the Track List. A • appears to indicate that the track is muted.

KC   Mute Objects «M»
KC   Mute Track «F1»
KC   Mute All Tracks of Folder «SH F1»
KC   Mute All Tracks With Same Instrument of Song «OP F1»
KC   Mute off for all
KC   Solo off for all

- Icons and large icons. (Enabling large icons allows the icon size to change as the track is zoomed vertically.)

Quick tip

You can create and use custom icons for Environment objects, which will also be used on Arrange tracks. They must measure 128 by 128 pixels and be in Portable Network Graphics (.png) format. To be recognized by Logic, a custom icon must be named ###.png, where ### is the desired position of the icon in the Instrument list. They must also be placed in a folder named Icons inside the EmagicResources folder. In OS 9 that is located in the same folder as the Logic application. In OS X it is located in ~/**Library**/**ApplicationSupport**.

- Track Instrument colour. (When enabled, a narrow bar in the colour of the Environment object assigned to the track appears at the right end of the Track List.)
- Track Instrument MIDI channel, Instrument name, and track name.

An important point to keep in mind is that the Track List influences the Mixer window (see Chapter 5) in the following ways:

- The top-to-bottom order of Tracks is reflected in the left-to-right order of channels strips in the Mixer.
- If two or more tracks use the same Instrument, the lowest one determines the mixer position.
- Instruments of hidden tracks are still displayed in the mixer.

Quick tip

When the track's vertical zoom is large enough, both the Instrument name and the track name will be displayed, with the Instrument name on top. When the zoom is not large enough, the checked item will be displayed. If both items are checked, both will be displayed separated by a vertical line.

Quick tip

As with all Arrange window display elements, the Track List options can be different for different Arrange windows.

Track List order and zoom

You can control the vertical zoom of individual tracks by click-dragging at the bottom-left corner of the track in the Track List. The cursor becomes an index finger in zoom mode. Holding the Command key will cause only tracks of the same type (MIDI or audio) to be zoomed. Clicking with the Shift key will return all tracks to their individual zoom settings.

KC   Zoom Vertical In (bigger) *«CT Down Arrow»*
KC   Zoom Vertical Out (smaller) *«CT Up Arrow»*
KC   Individual Track Zoom In *«CT OP Down Arrow»*
KC   Individual Zoom Vertical Out *«CT Up Arrow»*
KC   Toggle Individual Track Zoom *«CT OP F3»*
KC   Auto Track Zoom *«F3»*

Quick tip

You can also have individual tracks zoom automatically as they are selected. The auto-zoom amount is the last manual-zoom set for an individual track.

You can sort the Track List by MIDI channel, audio channel, output channel, track name, or Instrument name. If you don't like the results, undo immediately, because there is no 'sort by original order' option. Sorting applies only to the current view – if you're inside a Folder, only its tracks get sorted.

KC   Arrange » Functions » Track » Sort Tracks by …

The Parameter area

The Parameter area to the left of the Track list contains four important displays (from top to bottom): Region parameters, Toolbox, Instrument parameters, and Mixer Channel Strip (when appropriate). The Toolbox display can be suppressed from the View menu, and the Region and Instrument parameter boxes can be minimized by clicking the wedge at their top-left corner.

Region parameters

The parameters for MIDI Regions include offsets for MIDI note Velocity and pitch, various quantization settings and amounts, MIDI delay, gating, and dynamics, looping, and default score settings. An extended set of parameters can be viewed and edited by double-clicking on any text in the box. That opens a floating window with the additional parameters.

Quick tip

You can set Region parameters for a single Region, a multi-Region selection, or no selection. Changes made when multiple Regions are selected apply relatively unless the Option key is held, in which case all settings get the same value. Multiple Region selections can include Regions on different tracks. For MIDI tracks, when no Region is selected, the changes apply to MIDI thru and are used as the settings for all newly recorded Regions. Incoming MIDI data is recorded without modification, however.

The parameters for audio Regions control fade in/out, crossfading, delay, and looping. There are no extended parameters, but double-clicking will still open a floating window.

Instrument parameters

The Instrument Parameter Box, below the Toolbox, is the same Parameter Box that appears in the Environment window when an object is selected there. See Chapter 4 for details.

Arrange window tools

Figure 3.05
The Arrange window Toolbox has 12 tools for working with Regions and Automation. They can be selected using Key Commands or by clicking directly in the Toolbox.

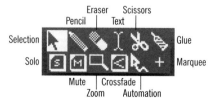

The Arrange window toolbox contains the following tools:

Selection: Select Regions by clicking or click-dragging. Add or remove Regions from the selection by Shift-clicking.

Quick tip

The resolution of click-dragging a selected Region or group of Regions depends on the Arrange window zoom. At low zoom settings (more objects visible) dragging snaps to bar lines. At higher settings dragging snaps to quarter notes. Hold the Control key to move by smaller note divisions. Hold Shift and Control to move by single ticks.

Pencil: Create MIDI Regions by clicking at the desired time position.

Quick tip

To add audio Regions directly from your hard drive to the Arrange window, hold Shift while clicking with the Pencil tool. The corresponding audio file will also be added to the Audio window.

Eraser: Delete Regions by clicking.
Text: Name Regions by clicking then typing in a name.
Scissors: Split MIDI and audio Regions by clicking at the desired split point.

Quick tip

Option click to divide the Region into equal-sized slices. Click-drag to scrub the audio or MIDI Region before splitting (by releasing the mouse button).

Glue: Click-drag to select. Click any selected Region to merge all selected Regions.

Quick tip

Attempting to merge non-contiguous audio Regions requires confirmation. You can glue MIDI Regions on different tracks, but audio Regions must be on the same track.

Solo: The Solo tool functions also as a scrub tool. Clicking a Region will cause playback of that Region to begin at the click point. Dragging will influence playback speed. If you stop dragging but continue holding the mouse button, playback will proceed at the normal rate. Scrubbing works for both MIDI and audio Regions (when supported by your audio hardware).

Quick tip

You can drag with the Solo tool to select multiple Regions. If multiple Regions are selected, all will play.

Quick tip

Show Tools opens the Toolbox under the cursor for quick selection of the desired tool.

Quick tip

There are also Key Commands for selecting each individual tool.

Mute: The Mute tool toggles muting of individual Regions.

Zoom: Click-dragging an area with the Zoom tool cause the window to zoom to fit that area vertically and horizontally. (See Chapter 2 for tips on zoom management.)

Crossfade: The Crossfade tool allows you to create crossfades between overlapping audio Regions.

Automation: The Automation tool is used to change the shape of automation segments using smooth exponential and S-shaped curves.

Marquee: The Marquee tool allows you to select a two-dimensional area in the Arrange window. All data in the selected area (including partial Regions) can then be moved, deleted, copied, etc.

KC   Show Tools *«ESC»*
KC   Set Next Tool
KC   Set Previous Tool

Quick tip

Selecting any tool with the Command key held down makes that tool an alternate tool. The cursor will thereafter change to that tool whenever the Command key is pressed.

Marquee tool tips

KC   Set Marquee Tool

The primary purpose of the Marquee tool is to allow you to select and operate on areas that enclose partial Regions. Here are some ways to use it:

• Select a multi-bar segment of MIDI and audio Regions for moving or copying to another location without having to slice and move the Regions individually.

Quick tip

Simply clicking within the selection area with the Selection or Scissors tool will cut all Regions touched by the selection at the selection borders. Loops will be turned to real copies so as to preserve their original contents. The first full Region created after the cut will have looping turned on. The idea is to preserve the original sound as much as possible.

Info

Aliases are handled differently than loops. Although they are cut at the selection boundaries, they are not turned to real copies and each new Alias refers back to the same original. That usually means the original sound is not preserved.

Quick tip

Note that the Selection and Marquee tools are adjacent in the Arrange toolbox. Assigning 'next tool' and 'previous tool' to convenient key commands makes switching between those tools easy.

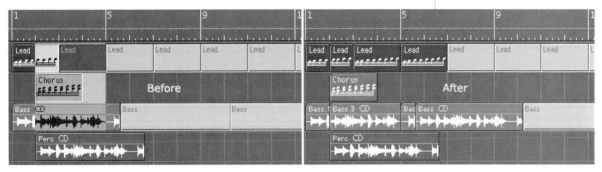

• Crop all Regions touched by a selection to include only those parts within the selection.

KC   Crop objects outside Marquee *«CT C»*

• Mute the portion of any Region within the selection and simultaneously split the Regions at the selection borders. You can use the key command or Mute tool to accomplish this after using the Marquee tool to make the selection.
• Set the locators to the selection borders.

M   Arrange » Functions » Objects » Set Locators by Objects
KC   Set Locators by Objects *«CT =»*
KC   Set Rounded Locators by Objects *«=»*

About Space and Time

Logic has a number handy features for splitting and combining Regions as well as cutting and inserting time in a song.

There are menu selections and key commands to split a single MIDI Region into multiple Regions containing only events on a single MIDI channel. That is useful when you've recorded different MIDI controllers (using different MIDI channels) on a single track, which is the only way to record multiple MIDI parts in a single pass. It's also useful when you've converted a polyphonic MIDI part to individual voices using the option found in Logic's various MIDI editors.

M   Arrange » Functions » Split/Demix » Demix by Event Channel
M   Editor » Functions » Note Events » Lines to Channels
KC   Demix by Event Channel *«CO D»*
KC   Lines to Channels

There is a menu selection to split a single MIDI Region into multiple Regions containing only notes of a single pitch. That's useful for percussion parts in which different pitches correspond to different drum sounds. It's a good idea to pack the original part into a Folder by itself, as this function can create a lot of separate tracks.

M   Arrange » Functions » Split/Demix » Demix by Note Pitch

Figure 3.06
Before and after selecting with the Marquee tool and clicking within the selected area. Note that Loops have been modified to preserve playback, the Region on the bottom track has not been affected because it was not within the selection, and the Region on the second track has not been affected because it was entirely within the selection.

Quick tip

You can accomplish the opposite result – leaving only the parts not within the selection – by deleting or cutting the selection with the Eraser tool or a key command.

There's a menu selection to cut the portion of all selected Regions that falls between the Left and Right Locators. The portions of the affected Regions outside the Locators will be moved to close up the gap. Unselected Regions will not be affected.

M   Arrange » Functions » Split/Demix »
KC Snip: Cut Time and Move by Locators *«<»*

There's a menu selection to insert an amount of time equal to the time between the Locators and simultaneously split selected Regions (placing empty space between them). Unselected Regions are not affected. If you want to insert an empty block of time in to the song, select all Regions before using this function.

M   Arrange » Functions » Split/Demix » Insert Time and Move by Locators
KC Insert Time and Move by Locators *«SH <»*

There are two methods of tying together Regions on the same track: by moving and by lengthening. Both methods work on multiple selections across multiple tracks, but tying occurs only between adjacent Regions on the same track. Tying by moving starts with the leftmost selected Region and moves each selected Region to its right until all selected Regions butt up against each other. Tying by lengthening, changes the length of each Region (including overlapping Regions) so that it butts up against the Region to its right. In the context of audio Regions, the lengthening is limited to the length of the audio file containing the Region.

M   Arrange » Functions » Object » Tie Objects by Position Change
KC Tie Objects by Position Change *«SH CT Tab»*

M   Arrange » Functions » Object » Tie Objects by Length Change
KC Tie Objects by Length Change *«CT Tab»*

KC Pickup Clock (Move Event to SPL Position)
KC Pickup Clock & Select Next Event
KC Goto Selection *«SH Space»*

M   Arrange » Functions » Copy MIDI Events
KC Copy MIDI Events *«R»*

Trash talk

Logic saves any deleted MIDI Regions along with their track assignment and time position in a Trash area, which looks exactly like the Arrange window. You can drag Regions from the Trash back into the Arrange window if need be. There is a Global preference to empty the trash each time the song is saved. If you don't enable it, you will need to empty the trash manually.

M   Arrange » Functions » Trash » Open Trash
M   Arrange » Functions » Trash » Empty Trash

Quick tip

You can move all selected Regions to the current SPL position while preserving their relative position with the Pickup Clock key commands. You can also move the SPL to the start of any selection.

Quick tip

You can perform complex copying and moving of MIDI data from multiple Regions using the Copy MIDI Events dialog. For example, you can make multiple copies of all MIDI events that fall between the Locators in selected Regions, starting at the SPL.

Quick tip

The Trash is a handy short-term backup for MIDI Regions, but is no substitute for backing up your work.

Miscellaneous tips

- If you have alternate takes for a part spread over several tracks and you have selected and sliced the portions you want to use, you can quickly move them to the same track with a key command:

KC   Move Selected Objects to Track

- There is a Global Preference to limit dragging to one direction (vertically or horizontally) in the Arrange window. Whether you choose to turn that feature on or off, the alternate state can be invoked by holding the Shift key while dragging. (Click-hold until the cursor becomes a hand before pressing the Shift key or you will invoke drag-selecting instead.)
- Ever ripped that perfect riff on your MIDI keyboard while playing along with Logic and wished you had been recording? Logic is always secretly recording its MIDI input and has a key command for capturing that missed take.

KC   Capture Last Take as Recording *«SH *»*
KC   Capture Last Take as Recording & Play

- You can drag Regions in the Arrange window without topping the window. The trick is to ensure that the mouse button is held for a while – short clicks top the window. The same tip applies to all windows.

The Environment

As mentioned in Chapter 1, Logic's Environment manages all MIDI and audio signal routing. In the case of MIDI, the data passes through the Environment on its way into and out of Logic and can be modified there. Audio data does not pass through the Environment, but Environment objects are used both for audio routing and for automation of mixing and plug-in settings. I'll start with a look at the essential MIDI and audio objects, then get into some more specialized MIDI processing possibilities.

MIDI outputs

Routing of MIDI messages to external MIDI devices, including other MIDI software running at the same time as Logic, is handled by four objects: three types of Instrument objects and an object designed for Rewire 2 communication.

Figure 4.01
Logic's four types of MIDI output object are shown here. Typically these objects are assigned to Arrange window tracks to transmit MIDI playback and incoming MIDI to external MIDI devices. The Multi-Instrument represents 16 separate, channelized MIDI outputs called sub-channels, and it is those that are usually assigned to tracks.

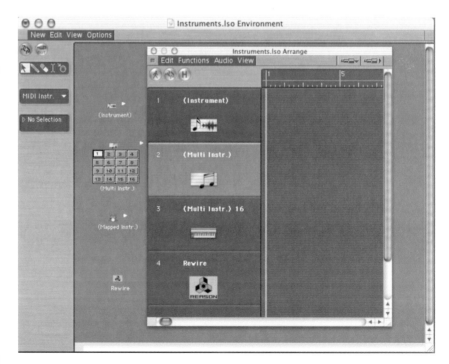

Each of those objects has an automatic connection (no cabling is required) to a MIDI port, which can be selected in the object's Parameter Box that appears at the left of the Environment window when the object is selected. Those objects can be used to send MIDI messages to MIDI ports in two ways: by cabling Environment objects into them that generate MIDI messages (Fader objects for example) and by assigning them to Arrange window tracks. In the latter case, data from MIDI Regions on the track – as well as incoming MIDI when the track is selected in the Arrange window – will be routed through them to their MIDI port.

Standard Instrument objects

This is Logic's most basic MIDI output object. It is designed to communicate with a single-channel MIDI device. Its Parameter Box (see Figure 4.02) is typical of all Instrument objects. Here's a quick rundown of its parameters:

Icon: this checkbox controls whether the Instrument appears on the Arrange window's Instrument pop-up menu, which is the easiest way to assign it to an Arrange track. You can also assign it to a track by dragging or using the Environment's MIDI tool.

Port: use this pop-up menu to select the Instrument's MIDI output port.

Cha: this sets the output channel and overrides the MIDI channel of the data being sent. Set it to All if you want to leave the channel unaffected.

Prg: the left numerical sets the bank and program number and the right numerical, the program number for MIDI program change messages. When the checkbox

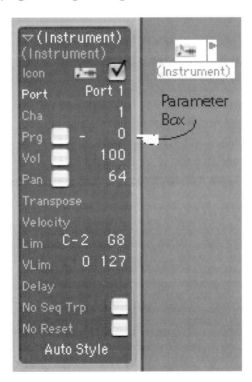

Figure 4.02
Each Environment object has a Parameter Box where you can control various aspects of the object's behaviour. Shown here are the parameters for the Instrument object.

is checked, MIDI bank and program change messages are sent whenever a track assigned to the Instrument is selected in the Arrange window. Otherwise, the settings are not used.

Vol: same as Prg, but for MIDI volume messages (controller #7).

Pan: same as Prg, but for MIDI pan messages (controller #10).

Transpose: sets a transpose amount in semitones for MIDI note messages. The range is ±96 semitones. Click closer to the word Transpose to select an octave transpose from a pop-up menu.

Velocity: sets a Velocity offset of up to ±99.

Lim: limits the pitch range within which MIDI notes will be transmitted to the port.

Vlim: limits the Velocity range within which MIDI notes will be transmitted to the port.

Delay: sets a delay of up to ±99 ticks for MIDI data being transmitted. This is useful for synchronizing MIDI devices which exhibit latency or have slow attack envelopes.

No Seq Trp: disables the transposition set in the Sequence Parameters. That is useful for drum parts, for which transposition would change the drum sound rather than its pitch.

No Reset: prevents automatic reset messages from being sent. That's useful when, for example, you want the MIDI Mod Wheel (controller #1) not to be reset on stops and cycle-jumps.

Auto Style: this menu allows you to select any score style to be used for MIDI Regions on this track. The default setting, Auto Style, selects a style deemed appropriate.

KC New Standard Instrument

Multi Instrument objects

The Multi Instrument object is essentially 16 Standard Instrument objects rolled into a single package. Each of these, called sub-channels, has a fixed MIDI channel and shares the same port, but all the other Instrument parameters can be set individually.

The purpose of the Multi Instrument object is to address multi-channel MIDI devices, which will receive MIDI data and play different sounds on separate MIDI channels. The numbered squares in the Multi Instrument icon can be clicked to activate individual sub-channels and the sub-channels Icon checkbox can be used to deactivate them.

Quick tip

Instrument objects make excellent MIDI outputs for Environment processes. Keep in mind that you can have more than one Instrument object assigned to the same MIDI port—thereby allowing you to use different Instrument parameter settings for different purposes.

Quick tip

MIDI messages cabled into the Multi Instrument are not automatically routed by their channel to the corresponding Multi Instrument sub-channel. To do that you need to Option-Click the outlet of the object that you want to cable to the sub-channel and select the sub-channel from the pop-up Instrument menu that appears. If you do that for each of the outlets of a Channel Splitter object (see below), you can then use the Channel Splitter to route incoming MIDI messages to the appropriate sub-channel.

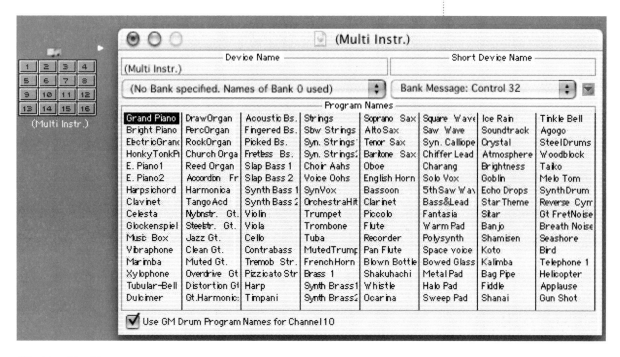

KC   New Multi Instrument

Mapped Instrument objects

The Mapped Instrument is designed for drums, but it has a number of unique features that also make it useful for creative MIDI processing. Each MIDI pitch can be mapped individually in the following ways:

- It can be assigned a different pitch.

Quick tip

Assigning different pitches allows you to, for example, assign two different keys to the same drum sound, making it easier to play flams and rolls.

Quick tip

When you want to remap pitches such that all octaves of the same pitch have the same mapping, it's easier to use a Chord Memorizer object as described below.

- It can be assigned a Velocity offset of up to ±127.
- It can be assigned its own MIDI channel.

Info

The note's channel is set in the *Base* column and is actually an offset of up to 16 to the Mapped Instrument's *Cha* parameter setting. If the resulting value is over 16, it is rolled over (17->1, 18->2, etc.)

Figure 4.03
One key advantage of the Multi Instrument is its ability to hold program names for up to 14 banks of 128 programs each. You can enter the names individually or paste whole name banks from the clipboard. That allows you to create and edit bank names in a word processor or spreadsheet program.

- It can be assigned its own cable outlet from the Mapped Instrument object. Up to 16 separate outlets are available.

Quick tip

You can use different outlets to map individual notes to different MIDI drum devices or to different Environment processes. The first time you draw a cable, you will be asked if you want to remove the default output assignment. That's usually what you want to do.

- It can be assigned its own notehead, position and grouping for scoring purposes.

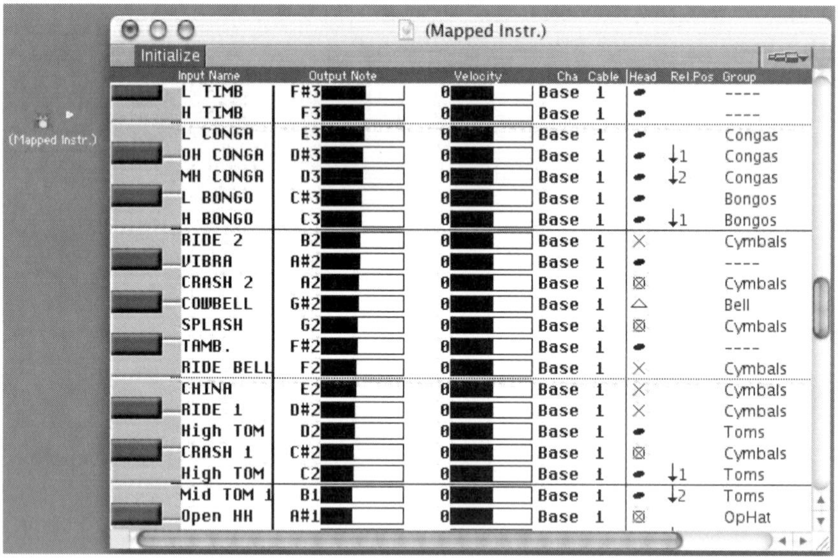

Figure 4.04
The Mapped Instrument's drum mapping window.

KC New Mapped Instrument

Audio objects

Although audio does not flow through Environment cables, Environment Audio objects are needed for audio recording, playback, instruments, and effects routing. Seven object types are provided, each with its own task.

KC New Audio Object

Info

When you create an Audio object from the Environment's New menu, it will appear as a small icon with the name Audio Object. Double-click it to reveal its full graphic as shown in Figure 4.05. You must also define its type using the *Cha* pop-up menu in its Parameter Box. The possible types are described below.

Audio Track objects

The term *track* has a confusing double-meaning in Logic, it refers both to the Audio objects used for routing audio Region playback to your audio outputs, and to the tracks in the Arrange window from which audio Regions are played. You need a different Audio Track object for each individual audio channel you wish to use. The maximum number you can have depends on your version of Logic.

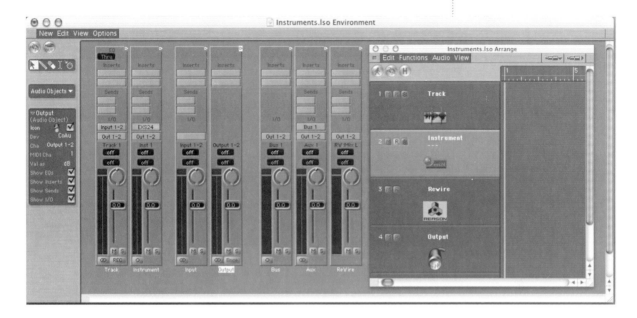

You can have several Arrange window tracks assigned to the same Audio Track object, but only one of them can be playing an audio Region at any given time. Still, multiple tracks for the same object can be handy for visually separating Regions that play over the same audio channel, and for using the same audio channel in different Folders.

Each Audio Track object has an optional Input and Output. The Input is for recording incoming audio and the output is for routing it to your audio interface. You might want to disable the output, for example, if you're using the Audio Track to feed a bus or a sidechain of an effect (a Vocoder, for example), and you don't want the audio on that channel heard directly.

Each Audio Track object can have up to eight sends, each routed to any of 32 (or optionally 64) send buses. Each send has its own level control and can be pre- or post-fader. Returns can be via Bus objects or Aux objects (see below). Each Audio Track object can also have up to 15 insert effects, in the unlikely event that you need that many.

Figure 4.05

Logic has seven Audio object types: Track (for Audio Region playback), Instrument (for audio instrument plug-ins), Input (to route incoming audio for recording), Output (to route audio to various Interfaces and ports), Bus (for send-effects returns), Aux (for more flexible bus routing), and Rewire (for routing Rewire audio into Logic). There is also a Master object (not shown) for controlling output volume for all outputs simultaneously.

Quick tip

Typically you would create Audio Track objects in your Autoload song's Environment for enough audio channels to cover your maximum required track count. There's no reason you can't add more in any given song, but other than screen real estate, there's also no reason not to have as many as you're likely to ever need in your Autoload Environment.

Quick tip

Both MIDI and audio Regions can be placed on Arrange tracks assigned to Audio Track objects. MIDI data will be routed to the channel strip and plug-in slots for automation. Audio data will be played by the Audio Track object.

Audio Instrument objects

You need an Audio Instrument object for each audio instrument plug-in you wish to use. Audio Instrument objects have the same slot configuration as Audio Track objects, with the one difference that the Audio Track object's Input slot is the Audio Instrument object's instrument plug-in slot. In OS 9 and on Windows, Emagic native plug-ins and VST plug-ins can be used. In OS X, Emagic native and Audio Unit (AU) plug-ins are supported.

Info

Only MIDI data will be recorded and played back on Arrange tracks assigned to Audio Instrument objects. All MIDI data except MIDI controller messages go directly to the audio instrument plug-in for playback. MIDI controller data will either be routed directly to the audio instrument plug-in or be split among the first four plug-in slots, depending on the Song Settings *Software Instruments Use* setting (see Chapter 1).

Info

Latency only applies to real time MIDI input, not MIDI playback.

Audio Instrument latency

Latency – the delay between when a note is played and when it sounds – is a crucial issue when using audio instrument plug-ins. A variety of factors contribute to latency including the design of the audio instrument plug-in, the audio interface, and audio and MIDI drivers. The one factor under your control, however, is the I/O buffer size, which is set in the Audio Hardware & Drivers Preferences. Lower settings result in lower latency and greater CPU load. Very low settings can result in distortion, and in some cases, crashes. As a rule of thumb, set this value as low as possible consistent with good performance.

In addition to the audio interface buffer size just mentioned, Logic always keeps one Audio Instrument object in what is called *Live* mode, which means it doesn't have to be activated each time a note is received. Live mode, which amounts to always keeping the plug-in active, results in a constant CPU drain, and that is why only on Audio Instrument object is kept in Live mode. The Audio Instrument object in Live mode is always the last one that was selected on an Arrange track.

Layering Audio Instruments

If you attempt to layer several audio instrument plug-ins by cabling a neutral Environment object such as a Monitor to each of their Audio Instrument objects and assigning that object to an Arrange track, only one of the Audio Instrument objects will be in Live mode. The others may exhibit extreme latency. Here is a trick to force more than one Audio Instrument object into Live mode:

• Insert an I/O plug-in from the Logic » Helpers section of the effects plug-in menu into the top effects slot of each Audio Instrument object that you wish to put in Live mode.
• Ensure that there is a real Input and Output assignment (not '—') for the I/O plug-in.
• Bypass the I/O plug-in.

The Audio Instrument object will now be kept in Live mode.

Quick tip

A quick way to layer Audio Instrument objects in Live mode is to enable the record button on each of their Arrange tracks. Then selecting any one of those tracks will route live MIDI input to all of them.

Audio Input objects

The purpose of the Audio Input object is to allow destructive processing of incoming audio data by insert and send effects. It also allows recording of incoming audio during real-time bouncing. (Obviously, offline bouncing, which happens faster that real time, does not accommodate real-time recording.)

Info

Audio Input objects are assigned to a specific mono or stereo hardware input in their Parameter Box. An output assignment can be made on their channel strip as with the Audio Track object and Audio Instrument object.

Audio Output objects

Audio Output objects control the output level and pan/balance for each output on your audio interface. Like the Input objects, they are assigned a specific hardware output in their Parameter Box.

Quick tip

Audio Output objects are the place to insert audio mastering plug-ins such as multi-band compression, EQ, and limiting that you want to apply to the total mix.

You can bounce the output of any Audio Output object to an audio file by clicking the object's *Bnce* button. That brings up the Bounce dialog, which allows you to record the mix of all un-muted tracks assigned to Audio objects routed to the designated output. You can set the bounce area, which by default is set to the area between the Left and Right Locators, choose whether to apply dithering, and choose between *Realtime* and *Offline* bouncing. Offline bouncing is faster, but doesn't allow you to apply live automation or record real time audio input.

Quick tip

You can bounce more than one output and bounce separate outputs to separate audio files by choosing Surround in the Bounce dialog.

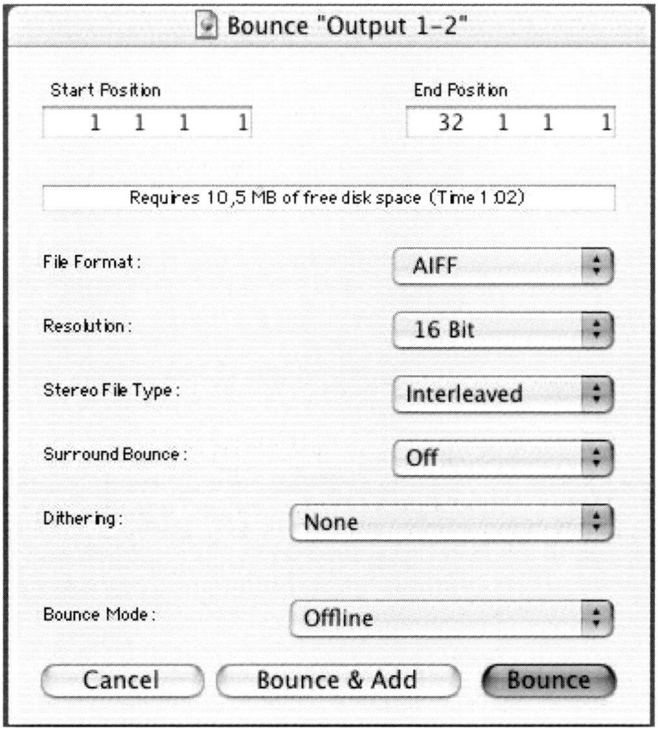

Figure 4.06
Logic's Bounce dialog pops up when you click the *Bnce* button on any Audio Output object.

Quick tip

If your purpose for bouncing is to retrieve CPU power and allow more tracks, instruments, or effects, consider Logic's Freeze function instead. It is faster, easier, and undoable on a per-track basis.

Audio Bus, Audio Aux and Audio Rewire objects

Audio Bus objects route the signal of individual send buses to audio outputs. Each Audio Bus object is set to a specific bus in its Parameter Box. They have slots for insert effects, but no sends of their own. The newer Audio Aux objects have made Audio Bus objects somewhat obsolete.

Audio Aux objects have a selectable input and output, insert slots, and their own sends. The available inputs include any bus, any audio input, and any output of a multi-channel instrument plug-in. You can have several Aux objects with the same input in order to apply separate, parallel processing. In short, Aux objects will do anything Bus objects will do and a great deal more.

Using Rewire

Logic provides two Environment objects for working with other Rewire applications: the Audio Rewire object and the Rewire Internal object. The former is for bussing the output of Rewire audio channels into Logic and the latter is for routing MIDI from Logic to other Rewire applications.

The Audio Rewire object functions exactly like the Audio Input and Audio Bus objects. Its Rewire input bus is selected in the Parameter Box, and it has a menu for selecting the audio output. It also has bus sends and effects plug-in slots. Rewire buses are always mono, hence so is the Audio Rewire object. You therefore need to use two objects for a stereo Rewire instrument.

The Rewire Internal object has three parameters:

Dev: selects the Rewire device to which it sends MIDI. All currently running Rewire software appears on the Dev menu.
Bus: selects the Rewire bus to use. This parameter's meaning depends on the Rewire receiving device. For Reason, bus 1 is the main MIDI input, Buses 2-5 are the four auxiliary Reason buses, and buses 6 and higher are used for individual devices in the Reason rack.
Cha: selects the channel on the selected bus. 16 channels are available per bus. For buses 6 and higher in Reason, the Cha menu will show the name of the target device in the Reason rack.

MIDI processing in the Environment

The Environment is made for MIDI processing. You can build very simple MIDI effects utilizing one or a few Environment objects as well as extremely complex effects with hundreds of objects and cables. I'll describe some simple effects that you can throw together in minutes.

Arpeggios, Delays, and Chords

The Arpeggiator, Delay Line, and Chord Memorizer objects are among the simplest to configure and use. You can use them for Arrange track playback or Arrange track recording (the configuration shown here). In either case, they can be used for MIDI-thru processing as well.

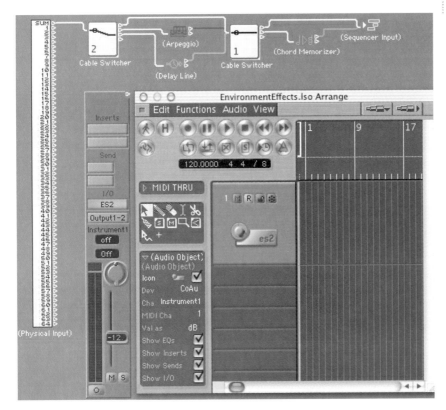

Figure 4.07
A simple input processing circuit for creating arpeggios, multi-tap delays, and chords. MIDI input is processed before being sent to the Arrange window for recording or MIDI thru. The Cable Switcher on the left selects among the Arpeggiator, Delay Line, and no processing. The Cable Switcher on the right selects between the Chord Memorizer and no processing. A couple of clicks and some simple Parameter Box setup allow you to create arpeggios and tap delays with or without chords.

The switching circuitry shown in Figure 4.07 allows you to switch between no processing (00), arpeggiation (10) or multi-tap delay (20) alone, arpeggiation (11) or multi-tap delay (21) followed by chord creation, and chord creation alone (01). (The numbers in parenthesis refer to the left switch position followed by the right switch position.)

The Cable Switcher is a special form of the versatile Fader object. In this form it is used to route MIDI messages to up to 128 separate destinations. As you cable an outlet, a new one is created below it for the next destination. The Cable Switcher can be set up to have its position controlled by incoming MIDI messages. In the illustration, its *In, Channel,* and *-1-* parameters cause it to be switched by incoming MIDI controller 81 messages on channel 1. The second Cable Switcher is controlled by MIDI controller 82, allowing those two controllers to select any processing combination.

Figure 4.08
The Parameter Boxes for the Cable Switcher, Arpeggiator, Delay Line, and Chord Memorizer objects. The Chord Memorizer's chord set-up window is shown in the middle. The result of processing the Delay Line output using the Chord Memorizer is shown in the score at the bottom (the input is ascending quarter-notes).

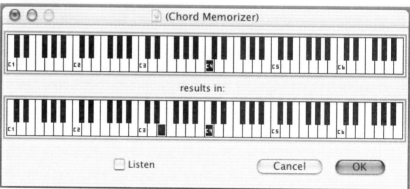

M   New » Fader » Specials » Cable Switcher

The Arpeggiator has parameters for arpeggio direction (Up, Down, Up & Down, Random, etc.), fixed Velocity, range of notes within which it applies (notes outside the range are passed through), arpeggiation rate (whole-notes to 768th notes or random), note length, snap value (waits to start arpeggio until the next occurrence), repeat (on/off), number of octaves, and Velocity crescendo (up to ±99). The *Ctrl Base* parameter sets up each of its other parameters for MIDI control. The value chosen is the MIDI controller number that affects the direction parameter. The remaining parameters are affected by successive MIDI controller numbers. In the illustration, MIDI control is turned off.

The Delay Line provides a multi-tap delay that can be set in increments of the current Transport Division setting (left numerical) and ticks (right numerical). You can choose the number of taps (up to 99) and set both a pitch transpose (up to ±96 semitones) and Velocity offset (up to ±99) for each successive tap. In the illustration, the Delay Line is set for two taps, one division apart, descending a major third, and decreasing in Velocity by 16 each step. You can choose whether to have the incoming (undelayed) MIDI note played or suppressed.

The Chord Memorizer maps single notes into chords. All notes related by an octave are mapped in the same way, meaning you only need to set chords for the notes in a single octave. When the Listen box is not checked, incoming MIDI notes select the source on the top keyboard and you click the desired chord notes on the bottom. When the Listen box is checked, you click to select the source and use incoming MIDI to set the chord.

The Chord Memorizers parameters include output channel (all incoming channels are processed), incoming note range to which it applies (default is C2 to C4), transpose for outgoing notes (Trp), a key-shift (Key), and a CableSplit option. The key-shift option shifts the incoming note down by the indicated amount, applies the chord, then shifts the outgoing notes up by the same amount. That preserves pitch intervals within the key, hence the name. The shift amount is indicated relative to the key of C. When CableSplit is on each chord note will be sent out a separate outlet. If there are too few cables, extra notes use the bottom outlet.

Quick tip

If you assign single notes instead of chords, the Chord Memorizer becomes a key map. That can be used for diatonic transposition. For example, map each white key to itself and each black key to the next-lower white key. Then set Trp to the desired transpose and set the Key to the same number of steps in the opposite direction. (Trp = +4 & Key=Ab to transpose a major third up, for example.)

Touch Tracks

Touch Tracks is one of the Environment's most powerful objects. It doesn't process MIDI data, doesn't use cables, and the parameters in its Parameter Box have no effect (they're a holdover from the Mapped Instrument). Touch Tracks is used for triggering individual MIDI Regions or Folders with a single MIDI note. The triggered Regions are played as if they were in their own Arrange window, therefore they should be muted in the Arrange window after being assigned to Touch Tracks key(s). Because it can trigger Folders, Touch Tracks can be used for arranging on the fly, and are great for live performance.

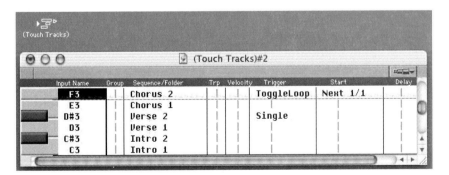

Figure 4.09
The Touch Tracks window sets up triggering of MIDI Regions and Folders by single MIDI notes.

When you create a Touch Tracks object, a window opens that looks much like the Mapped Instrument window. Drag MIDI Regions or Folders to the Sequencer/Folder column adjacent to the note number you wish to have trigger it. You can then set a transpose (for all MIDI note messages), triggering mode, Velocity offset (for all MIDI note messages), Start position (next whole, quarter, or

Quick tip

One of the most interesting features of the Delay Line is that if you cable more than one of its outlets, it will cycle the delays through successive cables. You could use that to play different sounds for each tap.

Info

The Delay Line affects all MIDI messages, not just notes. When that is not desirable (which it usually is not) use a Transformer to route other messages around the Delay Line.

Quick tip

Touch Tracks can only be used for MIDI data. You can not place audio Regions or Folders containing audio Regions in them. But you can use them to trigger audio instruments including samplers, so in that sense, they can be used for audio.

Quick tip

If you drag a MIDI Region or Folder to the Environment window, a Touch Tracks will automatically be created to play it from all MIDI notes, transposed relative to C3.

Quick tip

If you use a drum pad controller or a controller with single-click buttons, Gate mode is not a good choice.

sixteenth note), and Delay (up to ±999 ticks). Up to 99 Groups can be set up, to ensure that only one Region in any Group plays at a time.

Touch Tracks has three triggering modes: *Normal* (plays all the way through), *Gate* (plays as long as the note is held), and *Toggle* (the note toggles playback on and off). Gate and Toggle modes can be set to Loop or play once. Normal mode can be set to restart the Sequence/Folder *(Single)* or play multiple instances *(Multi)*.

Transformations

Figure 4.10
The Transformer object can be used to filter and transform MIDI messages in any way imaginable. The transformation shown will reverse a MIDI keyboard and change its velocity response.

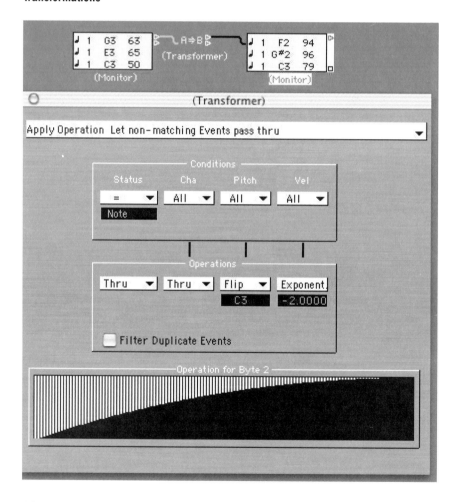

KC   New Transformer

The Transformer object can be used to filter, route, and modify any MIDI message type in numerous ways. It is a real time version of Logic's Transform window. The top section, labelled *Conditions,* is used to select which MIDI messages are affected, while the bottom section, labelled *Operations,* controls how those messages are modified. In the illustration, note messages have their pitch 'flipped' around Middle C while their Velocity is scaled exponentially according to the curve displayed at the bottom. The Monitor objects on either side of the Transformer show the incoming notes (left) and resulting outgoing notes (right). Here a C major triad (C3 E3 G3) is transformed to an F minor triad (C3 G#2 F2) – notice that the pitch-difference relative to C3 is preserved but inverted.

The Menu at the top of the Transformer window controls the Transformer mode and is one of its most powerful features. The default mode, shown here, allows other MIDI messages to pass through the Transformer unchanged. Alternatives include throwing them away, sending them out the second outlet, and several advanced-processing options. In the second illustration, note-on messages create new MIDI pan messages (controller #10), which are sent before the note. That causes pan position to track keyboard position.

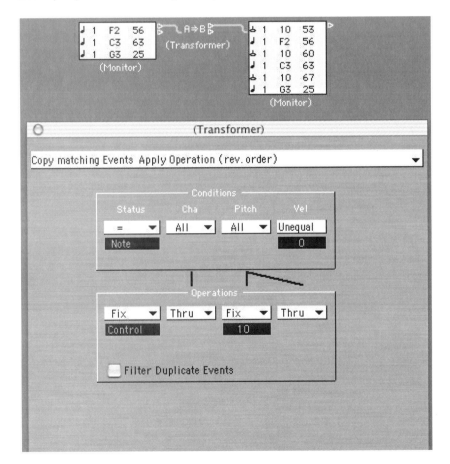

Figure 4.11
Here a Transformer is used to create MIDI pan messages that track incoming note-on pitches. High notes are panned to the right, while low notes are panned to the left. Notice the slanted line connecting the Pitch Condition to the rightmost Operation value. That transfers the pitch number to the pan value.

Quick tip

As with the previous example, the Transformer can be inserted at the input or cabled to an output object and assigned to an Arrange track.

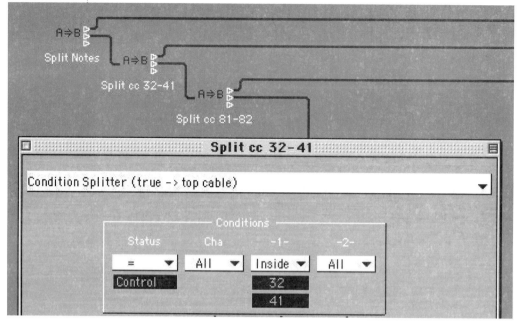

Figure 4.12
Transformer split routing for input processing. Only notes get processed. Controllers 81 and 82 are routed to the switches. Controllers 32 to 41 are routed to the Arpeggiator to control its parameters. Everything else goes directly to the selected Arrange track.

The Transformer's *Condition Splitter (true->top cable)* mode makes the Transformer a powerful routing device. You can use it with the *Arpeggio, Delay, and Chords* input processing circuit, for example, to ensure that only notes get processed as well as to route only those controllers to the Arpeggiator that affect its parameters.

Faders

The Environment offers a variety of styles and functions for its Fader object. Fader objects can be used to send MIDI messages to external MIDI devices, to create MIDI automation by recording onscreen changes on MIDI tracks, and to control other Environment objects. For example, any of Transformer Condition and Operation value can be set remotely using special messages called *Meta-messages* that can be generated by Fader objects.

Fader objects can also be controlled by incoming MIDI messages. As a consequence, they can be used to convert one type of MIDI message to another as can the Transformer. Whereas Faders can't change the converted message values, they do display the value onscreen and it can be changed with the mouse.

There are several special Faders that can be used to affect Logic's behaviour. With the exceptions of the Cable Switcher discussed above and an Alias Assigner (which I won't go into), the special Faders generate internal Logic messages called *Meta-messages*. Meta-messages do things like change Logic's tempo, change screensets (that's how you can access screensets with zero digits), jump Logic's SPL to Marker positions, and change parameters of other Environment objects.

Finally, there is the SysEx Fader, so called because it was originally intended for sending MIDI System Exclusive (SysEx) messages. However, the SysEx Fader is actually an Event list within a Fader, and can be used to send multiple MIDI messages of any kind, with or without changing of their values.

Table of Meta-messages for the Environment

Meta	Description
46	Fader becomes Alias Assigner (in Fader Out definition).
47	Send one 8-bit MIDI byte (in sequences only).
48	Fader becomes Cable Switcher (in Fader Out definition).
49	Jump to Screenset (Screenset number is Fader value).
50	Select Song MIDI message (to other MIDI devices).
51	Jump to Marker (Market number is Fader value).
52	Stop Playback.
96	Set Fader range minimum (when received by a Fader).
97	Set Fader range maximum (when received by a Fader).
98	Set Fader without sending (when received by a Fader).
99	'Bang' – send Fader value (when received by a Fader).
100	Temporary Tempo (BPM is Fader value plus 50).
122	Set Transformer Map value (when received by a Transformer).
123	Set Transformer Map position (when received by a Transformer).
124	Set all Condition maximums (when received by a Transformer).
125	Set all Condition minimums (when received by a Transformer).
126	Set all Operation maximums (when received by a Transformer).
127	Set all Operation minimums (when received by a Transformer).

Other useful objects

The Environment contains several utility objects to make life easier:

Channel Splitter: routes MIDI messages to separate outlets according to their MIDI channel.
Keyboard: displays currently held notes on a piano-keyboard. The keyboard can also be clicked to generate notes.
Monitor: a resizable list-display. Although it can be sized arbitrarily large, at most 32 messages will be displayed. After that the messages wrap around the top.
Ornament: a resizable box that can be used to graphically separate groups of objects. The Ornament can also be used as a cable junction – MIDI messages pass through to all its outlets without being affected.
GM Mixer: a 16 channel MIDI mixer. This is somewhat obsolete as individual MIDI channel strips appear in the Adaptive Mixer.
Voice Limiter: limits the number of simultaneous held MIDI notes by automatically turning off notes with selectable top, bottom, or last note priority.

Exchanging Environments

The Environment's Options menu offers a number of ways to import all or part of the Environment from one song into another. Those are accessed from the Import Environment sub-menu and the options are:

Layer: Imports all objects on a single layer from the source song and places them on a new layer in the target song. This is the most reliable form of importing, but you lose all connections between objects on other Environment Layers.
Custom: Allows you to specify, on a per-object basis, which objects from the source song replace which objects in the target song. This is the most complex option, but it gives you the most control over the results.
Merge: Adds all objects from the source song to the destination song.
Update: Same as Merge, except objects with the internal ID are replaced. Since you can't see the internal ID, you're never sure what you're going to get.
Replace by Port...: Replaces only objects that have similarly named objects in the source Environment. The names must be a close, but not exact match.
Replace by Name: Replaces only objects that have similarly named objects in the source Environment. The names must be a close – an exact match is not required.
Total Replace: Deletes everything in the target. Replaces only objects that have similarly named objects in the source Environment. The names must be a close, but not exact match.

The Mixer window

ogic's Adaptive Track Mixer is a highly configurable, onscreen mixing con-
sole that can be used for any combination of audio and MIDI tracks. You can
use it for static changes or to enter automation in real time. Key things to
remember about the Mixer are:

- The left-to-right order of its channel strips is controlled by the top-to-bottom
  order of Arrange window tracks.
- If two or more Arrange window tracks are assigned to the same Environment
  object, the lowest one will determine the position of the corresponding channel strip in the Mixer.

M   Mixer » Tracks » Same Instrument Tracks

- Mixer channel strips for Audio objects contain the same controls and insert
  slots as the Environment objects themselves.
- Mixer channel strips for MIDI Instrument objects offer audio-style mixing
  options including access to up to five MIDI controllers.
- Mixer channel strips are exactly duplicated in the parameters section of the
  Arrange window for the selected Track. You can do one-off mixing and
  automation there without opening a Mixer window.

KC   Open Track Mixer *«CO 2»* (as float *«OP CO 2»*)
KC   Toggle Track Mixer

Quick tip

There is an option on the Mixer's
Tracks menu to display multiple
channel strips for multiple tracks
assigned to the same object.

Quick tip

Like most Logic windows, the Mixer window can be opened as a normal or floating window. Since there are no key
commands that apply to the Mixer window and no Mixer tools, it generally makes sense to open it as a floating
window.

Audio Channels

Channel strips for any type of Audio object can be displayed in the Mixer window.
They have the same controls and slots as the corresponding Environment objects,
but the Mixer window is a more convenient display than an Environment window
because it reflects the Arrange window track assignments.

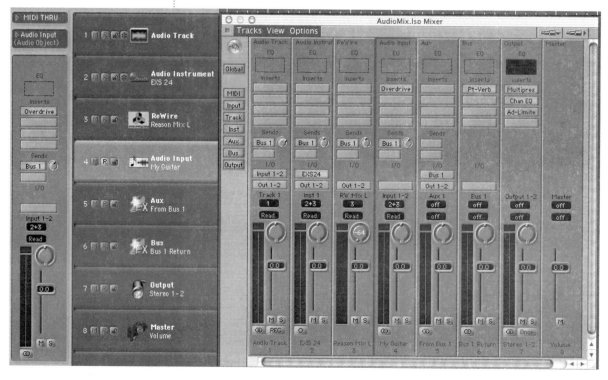

Figure 5.01
Any type of audio object can be displayed and controlled in the Mixer window. When a track assigned to that object is selected, the same channel strip appears in the Arrange window's parameter area at the left. You can use either to control available parameters as well as create automation.

You can use the buttons at the left of the Mixer window to control which object types are displayed. Display is on when the button has a blue background and off when it has a grey background.

- When multiple buttons are on, click any button to show only its object type.
- When multiple buttons are on, shift-click any button to add or remove its type from the display without affecting the other buttons.
- When only one button is on, click it to turn all buttons on or Shift-click it to turn all buttons off.

As in other Logic windows, you can hide the parameters to gain more display space.

M   Mixer » View » Parameters

Soloing and muting Audio Channels

Notice that there are Mute and Solo buttons below the volume slider on each audio channel strip, both in the Mixer and the Arrange window. These buttons work as exactly as they do on hardware audio mixing desks – they cause the audio from some channels to be disconnected from the output. Muting a channel causes its audio to be disconnected and soloing a channel causes all not-soloed channels' audio to be blocked.

Muting or soloing a channel with the buttons on the channel strip differs in several important ways from muting Arrange tracks or soloing Regions with the Solo and Mute tools or the Transport's Solo button:

- Muting from the channel strip does not stop the processing of audio Regions or plug-ins and therefore does not save CPU usage.
- Because audio processing continues, unmuting from the channel strip is instant, whereas there can be a delay while processing is restarted when objects are unmuted on Arrange tracks.
- Muting a channel strip mutes audio Regions on all Arrange tracks assigned to the corresponding Audio object, whereas muting in the Arrange window only affects selected tracks or Regions.

- *KC* Toggle (Mute) Audio Inputs
- *KC* Toggle (Mute) Audio Tracks
- *KC* Toggle (Mute) Audio Aux
- *KC* Toggle (Mute) Audio Outputs

Figure 5.02
Mixer channel strips for MIDI objects can display a variety of MIDI data. Options are controlled from the Mixer's **View** menu.

MIDI Channels

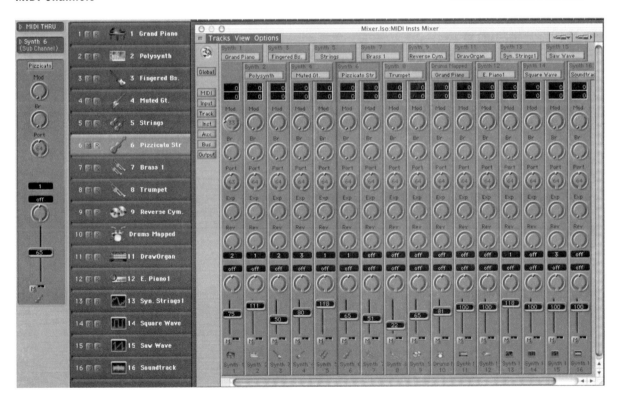

Mixer channel strips for MIDI Instruments (which are toggled with the MIDI button) offer a number of display options.

Figure 5.03
Mixer channel can be grouped together to achieve a variety of effects including grouped control settings, group automation, group display options, and group editing.

- Up to five MIDI controller knobs can be displayed. Select which of the five are displayed with *View » Assign #*.
- Click on the name above the MIDI controller knobs to assign which MIDI controllers they target. A drop-down menu will allow you to choose MIDI controllers 1 through 120 or one of 11 MIDI RPN messages.
- You can turn on MIDI program display and selection with *View » Program*. That will display a drop-down menu of the program names contained in the banks of the Multi-Instrument window. If the channel strip is for a Standard Instrument, the standard General MIDI (GM) names will be used. Use the menu to select programs by name.
- You can turn on MIDI program bank display and selection with *View » Bank*. That will allow you to make MSB/LSB bank selections. If you have set up Custom Bank Messages, those will be used.

Grouping Channel Strips

Mixer channels of any type can be assigned to one or more of up to 32 different Groups. Grouping allows linked control changes and automation, synchronized view options, and common range selections with the Marquee tool.

Groups are assigned using the Groups drop-down menu with the yellow display above the Pan knob. (The drop-down menu with the blue display is for automation settings—see Chapter 10.)

- Assign a channel strip to a Group by selecting it from the Group drop-down menu in the Mixer window or the Arrange window.
- A channel strip can be assigned to additional Groups by choosing them from the drop-down menu while holding the Shift key.

You control what actions are linked for a Group using the Group Settings window (see Figure 5.03), which can be opened from the Group drop-down menu or using a key command. You can also name Groups and enable/disable Group linking in the Group Settings window.

KC   Open Group Settings

The Group settings are self-explanatory with the possible exception of *Arrange Selection (Edit)*. When that is enabled, selecting any area on a grouped track using the Marquee tool will cause the same area to be selected on all tracks in the group. That can be a real time-saver as well as safety factor.

KC   Toggle Group Clutch

Group automation

When you create automation for a grouped setting such as volume, separate automation will be created for each track in the group that is in one of the write-automation modes (Touch, Latch, or Write). You can, therefore, later disable the group without losing the automation.

Using Folders for Mixer views

When the Mixer window is in Contents Link mode (yellow Link button), selecting any Folder will automatically switch the Mixer view to show channel strips for the tracks in the Folder. The object display buttons still apply in Contents Link mode.

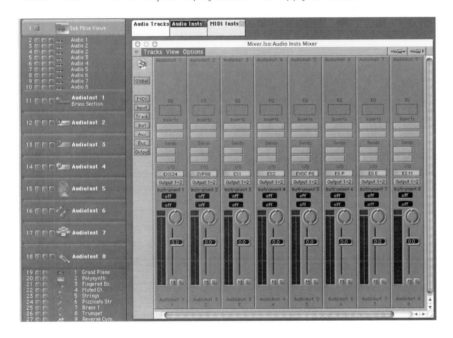

Figure 5.04
You can use empty Folders to hold Mixer views by ensuring the Folder contains all the tracks to be displayed in the view.

Automation

Logic offers two forms or automation: Track Based (TBA) and Region Based (RBA). RBA uses standard MIDI control change messages, which are contained directly in the Region regardless of its type (audio or MIDI). In the case of audio Regions, you can view and edit the MIDI data by opening the audio Region in any of the MIDI editors. TBA is not contained in specific Regions, but it can be viewed and edited in a list-style editor when necessary. Normally, you will view and manipulate it graphically directly in the Arrange window.

KC Automation Event Edit... *«CT CO E»*

Figure 6.01
Logic's Track and Region based automation can both be viewed and edited in a list-style editor and can both be created graphically as well as with onscreen or hardware sliders. The top Region and right Event editor show RBA MIDI data entered with Hyper Draw. The bottom Region and left Event editor show TBA Fader data entered with Hyper Draw.

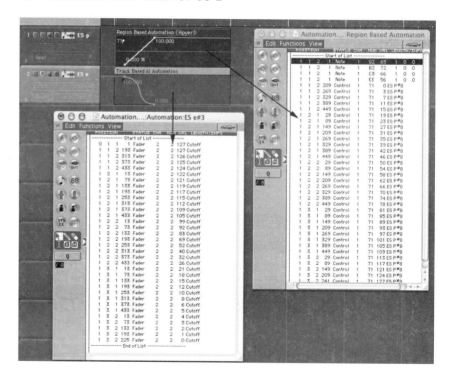

TBA for Audio plug-in automation (both instruments and effects) uses special events called Fader messages which are internal to Logic. TBA for MIDI devices and channel-strip automation uses standard MIDI control change messages.

M   Options » Track Automation » Move Current Track Automation Data To Object
KC   Move Current Track Automation Data To Object *«CT CO Down Arrow»*

Why two?

TBA is most like automation found on hardware mixing desks. It is time based, and probably the most useful and natural method for standard mixing tasks. It is also Logic's preferred method of automation for several reasons:

- TBA is sample accurate.
- TBA recording is independent of Logic's play/record status.
- TBA offers three recording modes: Touch, Latch, and Write.

RBA is the only method available for creating standard MIDI automation using MIDI controller messages. It is also the most natural method for controlling synthesizer and plug-in parameters that you want tied to other MIDI events such as notes.

M   Options » Track Automation » Track Automation Settings.
KC   Track Automation Settings *«OP A»*

Region Based Automation

RBA is really nothing more than standard MIDI data (other than notes) contained in MIDI Regions. It can be recorded using a hardware MIDI controller or an onscreen Environment Fader; it can be drawn in using Hyper Draw in the Arrange, Matrix, and Hyper Editor windows; and it can be entered and edited numerically in

Quick tip

You can transfer TBA Fader messages into Regions or you can force TBA data to move along with the Regions residing beneath it without actually transferring the data to those Regions.

Figure 6.02
Four views of RBA data: Arrange window Hyper Draw (top), Event editor (left), Matrix editor Hyper Draw (upper-right), and Hyper Edit window (lower-right). The data can be modified in the Arrange window or any of the editors shown here.

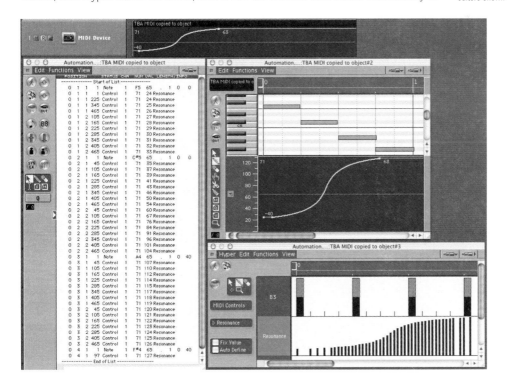

the Event editor window. Although RBA is usually thought of as MIDI controller data, other non-note MIDI messages such as pitchbend, channel pressure, and aftertouch can also be entered in each of those ways.

M   Arrange » Functions » Object » Lock SMPTE Position
M   Editors » Functions » Lock SMPTE Position
M   Arrange » Functions » Object » Unlock SMPTE Position
M   Editors » Functions » Unlock SMPTE Position
KC   Lock SMPTE Position «SH CT Down Arrow»
KC   Unlock SMPTE Position «SH CT Up Arrow»

Logic uses its own routing scheme for MIDI controller messages received by Audio objects. The following conventions are important to keep in mind when using RBA on tracks assigned to Audio objects:

- MIDI controllers 0 through 63 go to the channel strip and not to any plug-ins except as noted below.
- MIDI controllers 64 through 127 are sent in groups of 16 to the first four insert slots. If one of those slots is empty, its share of the controllers go to the slot immediately above.
- MIDI controllers used by a plug-in slot are assigned to plug-in parameters in the order they are shown when the Controls view of the plug-in control panel.

Figure 6.03
The Controls view of the Fat EQ plug-in control panel. This plug-in is inserted in the top slot of an Audio track and its controls will be automated by MIDI controller numbers starting with 64 for Band 1, 65 for Mode 1, 66 for Frequency 1, etc.

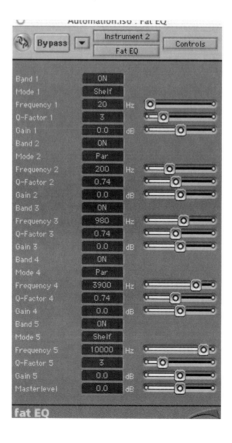

- For Audio Instrument objects, MIDI controllers 64 to 79 are always reserved for the Instrument slot, whether there is an Instrument plug-in installed or not.

Quick tip

There is an option in **File » Song Settings » Old Song** to pass all MIDI controllers directly through to the instrument plug-in slot. In that case the controller assignments set up by the plug-in designer are used. Many plug-ins have a MIDI Learn function that allows you to control the assignments.

M Arrange » View » Hyper Draw » Other …
KC Hyper Draw: Other «*SH F12*»

Track Based Automation

TBA is recorded directly on Arrange tracks, without reference to Regions residing on those tracks (no Regions need be present). Furthermore, whether and how recording takes place and whether existing automation is played back is dependent on the track's automation mode, which is set in its channel strip and is independent of Logic's record/playback state.

Quick tip

You can use TBA to control audio instrument and effects plug-in parameters during real-time recording of MIDI or audio.

Info

MIDI controller 64 is always reserved for MIDI Sustain Pedal messages and therefore can't be used to automate other Audio Instrument plug-in parameters.

Quick tip

If you use the Hyper Draw selection dialog to select the MIDI controller to be drawn on an audio track, the MIDI controller assignments will be displayed in the menu, relieving you of having to count which MIDI controller numbers go to which plug-ins.

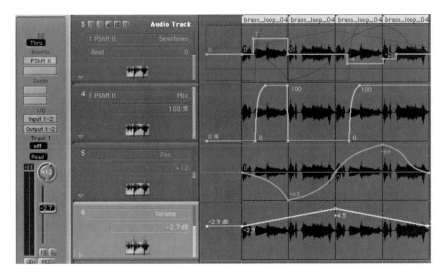

Figure 6.04
Track Based Automation lanes of four parameters of a single audio track. The top two lanes automate plug-in parameters and the bottom two automate volume and pan.

TBA is displayed as an overlay of the Regions on the track. The display can be toggled on and off. When TBA is displayed the Track list contains a menu for selecting the parameter for which automation is displayed (many parameters can be automated on the same track), a menu for selecting the automation mode, and a numerical and slider for recording automation (see Figure 6.05).

Figure 6.05
When TBA is visible, the Track list contains controls for setting up and recording automation.

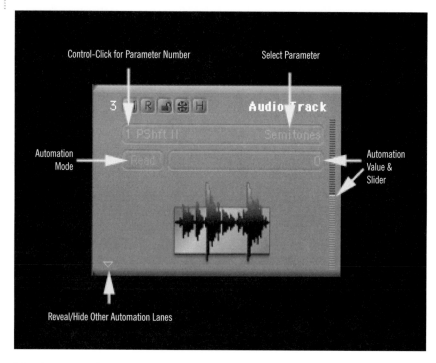

M   Arrange » View » Track Automation
KC   View Track Automation «*F4*»

If the track display is zoomed vertically, TBA for all parameters will be displayed in the background, with automation for the selected parameter highlighted and editable. You can also create lanes for other automation data on the same track by clicking the triangle at the lower-left corner of the track info area. Option-clicking will reveal and hide lanes for all automation present.

Creating Track Based Automation

Automation can be created graphically with the mouse or recorded in real time using onscreen controls or an external hardware controller (see below). The Arrange window's Selection and Automation tools are used for entering automation graphically:

- Click anywhere in an automation lane to create an automation breakpoint. You can drag the breakpoint to the desired value as you create it.
- Click an existing breakpoint to delete it.
- Shift-click and drag to select a multiple automation breakpoints. Then click-drag anywhere in the selected area (it will be shaded) to move all automation vertically or horizontally.

A supported hardware control surface, a standard MIDI controller, and the slider at the right of the track info area can be used to record automation in real time. There are three TBA record modes:

Quick tip

It's a good idea to leave TBA display off when you're not creating automation, because automation becomes the focus of the mouse when the cursor is in an automation lane, and you can easily create unwanted automation.

Quick tip

You can control the visibility of other automation data as well as the transparency of underlying Regions in Logic's Display Preferences.

Touch: Automation is written as long as the onscreen automation slider is being touched (i.e. while the mouse is down). When creating automation with MIDI input, writing 'times out' after a period of no incoming data.

Latch: Once the onscreen slider is moused or incoming automation data is received, automation continues to be written until Logic's transport is stopped.

Write: All automation for the track (not just the selected automation parameter) is erased as the SPL passes over it and new automation is recorded as received.

Quick tip

You can use a single MIDI controller to write all automation with Logic's Quick Automation Access feature. Once a controller is selected (see Figure 6.08) it can be used to write automation for whatever parameter is set up in the selected automation lane. For example, you could use your synth's Mod Wheel to quickly create automation.

Quick tip

Write mode is not advised. You can accomplish the same thing without danger of deleting other automation data using Touch or Latch mode. Deleting automation, when desired, is easily accomplished from a menu or with a key command.

Quick tip

The MIDI automation mode setting allows the onscreen slider to be used for recording Region Based Automation using standard MIDI messages.

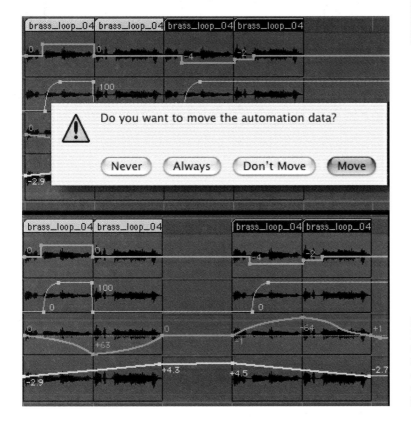

Figure 6.06
Moving Regions beneath TBA brings up a dialog with options to move or not move the underlying automation data. The Never and Always buttons can be used to suppress the dialog. The result of moving the automation is shown at the bottom.

Using MIDI controllers to create TBA

If you want to use a MIDI hardware controller surface to create TBA, but your hardware is not one of the supported controllers, you need to invoke some Environment trickery to get the job done. In short, you need to convert the incoming MIDI controller messages to Logic's special Fader messages and use a special Transformer mode to route them to the Audio object assigned to the TBA track. Figure 6.07 shows the details.

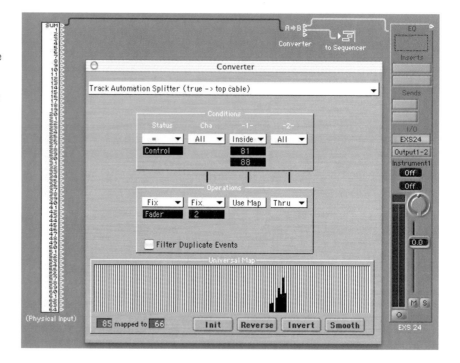

- Insert a Transformer between the Physical Input and the to Sequencer objects on the Environment's Clicks & Ports Layer. Cable the top outlet of the Transformer to the Audio object assigned to the Arrange track for which you want to create TBA. In Fig 7 that is an Audio Instrument object holding an EXS24 plug-in. Cable the second Transformer outlet to the to Sequencer object.
- Open the Transformer window and set its Conditions to select MIDI Controller messages for the MIDI controller numbers you wish to use for TBA. In Fig 7 MIDI controllers 81 through 88 are selected. Those will go to the Audio Instrument object. All other MIDI messages will go to the to Sequencer object.
- Set the Transformer's Status Operation to Fader. Set its Cha operation to 2 for automating the instrument plug-in slot. (Set it to 1 to automate the channel strip itself. Set it to 3 or higher to automate the effects slots counting from the top down.)
- Set the Transformer's -1- Operation to Use Map. For the selected controller numbers, set the map values to match the Fader message numbers needed for TBA. The easiest way to find that out is to cable the Audio object into a Monitor object, then change the settings on the plug-in's control panel. The Message number you see in the Monitor is the one needed for TBA of that control.

Moving TBA with Regions

You may or may not want your Track Based Automation to be moved as you move Regions around on an automated track. The Automation Settings window allows you to set up how Logic behaves under those circumstances: always move it, never move it, or ask. It also allows you to select which kinds of parameters automation can be written for. When a parameter type, such as volume, is turned off, you can create and playback automation graphically, but not with hardware or onscreen controllers.

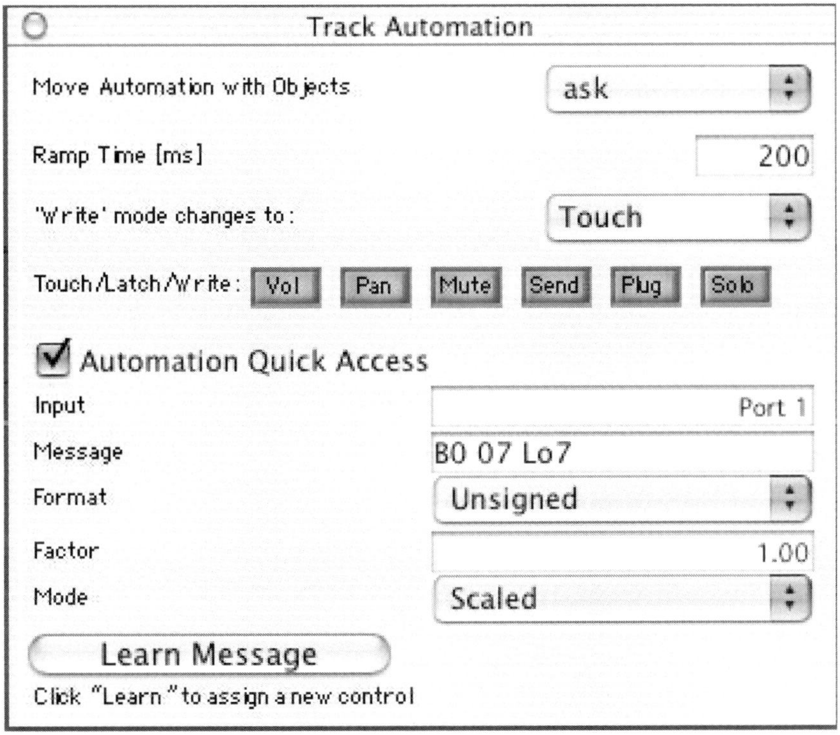

Quick tip

The method described here will allow you to create TBA for several parameters at a time. The downside is that you need to change the Transformer settings as well as its top cable destination to write TBA for a different track and plug-in. Quick Automation Access (described above) is usually easier.

Figure 6.08
The Track Based Automation dialog allows you to control various automation default settings. The menu at the top determines Logic's behaviour when you move a Region beneath existing automation (see Fig 6). The buttons in the centre enable/disable recording automation (you can still draw it in). The bottom section is for setting up Quick Automation

M   Options » Track Automation » Track Automation Settings…
KC   Track Automation Settings… «OP A»

Tempo, loops and grooves

Logic contains several tools for controlling the tempo and rhythmic groove of your music. The audio and MIDI domains, of course, offer different alternatives, and one of the keys to effective groove control is integrating the two. To that end it's worth taking a quick look at Logic's management of meter (bars and beats), time, and tempo.

Logic's Bar Ruler, which appears at the top of all time-oriented windows, displays meter (bars and beats) and can be set to also display time – select 'SMPTE Time Ruler' from the local View menu. Tempo, which is usually indicated in beats per minute (BPM), is the link between time and meter – changing the tempo causes the time to 'slide' relative to the meter marks.

KC   Position/Time Ruler in SMPTE units «U»

Figure 7.01
Logic's Bar Ruler shows the relation between meter (bars and beats) and time. The Tempo setting controls that relationship, and changing the tempo causes the time to "slide" relative to the meter marks.

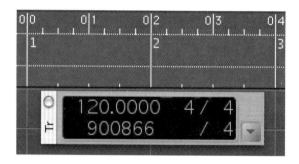

When you place any object (MIDI event, MIDI Region, audio Region, Folder, etc.) in a time-oriented window, it is anchored to the meter position. Therefore, its time position changes when the tempo is changed. (Of course, tempo changes can occur anywhere and only those before the object have any effect on its position.)

Info

It is a common misconception that audio Regions are anchored to time positions rather than meter positions. Only their length is fixed in time, their positions are anchored to meter position.

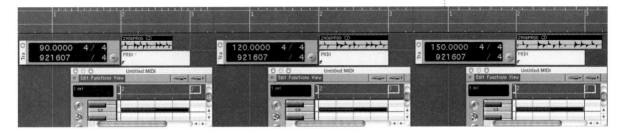

You can choose to anchor any object to its time-position rather than its meter-position by choosing 'Lock SMPTE Position' from the *Functions » Object* menu in the Arrange window and from the Functions menu in any of the Editor windows. Occasions when you might want to do that include:

- Dialog or sound effects audio Regions when you are working to picture.
- MIDI Regions when you want to change the tempo for scoring purposes without changing the real tempo.
- MIDI Regions or events when you want to insert tempo changes to align them to meter marks. (See ReClocking Your Song below.)

KC   Lock SMPTE Position
KC   Unlock SMPTE Position

Figure 7.02
The effect of tempo changes on MIDI notes and audio Regions. At 120 BPM (centre) the MIDI note event and audio Region are both one measure long. At tempos 90 and 150 the meter-length of the audio Region is changed, while its time-length stays the same. At all tempos, the MIDI note's meter-length stays the same, while its time-length changes with tempo.

Tempo synchronization

Many plug-ins and MIDI devices can synchronize their timed processes such as LFO rates, delay times, and envelope breakpoint grids to a host's tempo. They do the mathematics of converting note values to time values, but it doesn't hurt to know what's under the hood. Here are the relevant details:

- Logic's tempo, measured in beats-per-minute (BPM), is always relative to quarter note beats – it does not change with the time signature. For example, 120 BPM means 120 quarter notes per minute in both 4/4 and 6/8.
- Divide the BPM into 60 to calculate seconds per quarter note. Multiply that by 1,000 (i.e. divide BPM into 60,000) to calculate milliseconds per quarter note. Milliseconds are commonly used to set delay times less than a second. For example, at 120 BPM a quarter note lasts 60,000/120 or 500 ms.
- The easiest way to calculate the time for other note values is to first multiply the quarter-note time by four, which gives the time per whole note, then divide that by the note value. 120 BPM equates to 500 ms per quarter note and therefore, 2,000 ms per whole note. The time for a 16th note is then 2,000/16 or 125 ms.
- To calculate the frequency (for LFOs for example) for a given tempo, divide the BPM by 60. That gives you the number of quarter notes per second, and therefore, the frequency that equates to one cycle per quarter note. For other note values, first divide the quarter note frequency by four, then multiply by the note value. For example, at 120 BPM the frequency for quarter notes is 2 Hz which equates to 0.5 Hz for whole notes. For 16th notes, it is therefore 0.5 x 16 or 8 Hz.

Working with tempo

Logic has three tempo editors: List, Graphic, and Operations. The Tempo List works much like Logic's Event editor, allowing you to enter tempo changes and edit them numerically. The Graphic Tempo Editor is like Logic's HyperEdit window. You can use it to enter or edit tempo changes graphically with the mouse. The Tempo Operations window will generate tempo changes between two locations using a variety of mathematical curves.

Figure 7.03
Logic's Tempo List (left), Graphic Editor (lower-right), and Tempo Operations windows allow you to edit tempo changes numerically, by drawing with the mouse, and by using pre-defined curves.

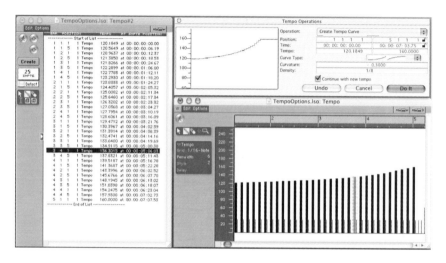

Quick tip

Whenever experimenting with tempo changes, especially when using ReClock song or Tempo Operations, it's a good idea to do so in a new tempo list. You can copy and paste between alternative tempo lists.

Quick tip

Logic maintains up to 10 completely independent tempo lists, called Tempo Alternatives. That allows you to experiment freely with tempo changes without travelling down a road of no return.

KC   Open Tempo List *«OP T»*
KC   Set Tempo Alternative

Quick tip

If you have MIDI sliders on your MIDI keyboard or have a hardware controller surface, you can set the In Definition of the Tempo Fader to match one of the sliders and control tempo remotely from your keyboard.

Remote tempo control

Logic has a special Meta-message (100) for temporarily setting Logic's Tempo. The resulting tempo is the Meta-message value plus 50, making the BPM range 50 to 177. The tempo resets whenever playback is stopped or there is a cycle jump.

You can record Tempo changes using this Meta-message by creating a Fader in the Environment and cabling it between the Physical Input and the to Sequencer object. (See Chapter 4 for details on Meta-messages and Environment objects.) The tempo changes are recorded in the current Tempo Alternative.

ReClocking your song

Logic's ReClock Song operation is most useful for automatically inserting tempo changes to align MIDI or audio whose tempo varies, to Logic's meter grid. Though the implementation can seem puzzling, the concept is easy to grasp if you imagine doing it manually (which is an extremely tedious process).

Suppose you have a sequence of quarter notes played at uneven tempo. When you place the sequence in the Arrange window and open it in a MIDI editor, the notes will not be aligned to Logic's quarter note grid lines. We've seen that you can lock in their time position by using Logic's Lock SMPTE Position option either on the sequence or the individual notes. Once they are locked into position, changing the tempo will change their position relative to the meter grid, but not in time. You could align them to the quarter note grid lines by inserting a tempo change at each quarter note and adjusting it until the next quarter note lines up. In a nutshell, that is what ReClock Song does automatically – it locks all data within the area being ReClocked and inserts tempo changes to align individual events to grid lines. The things you need to choose are:

- The events to be aligned to the grid. Those are called guide notes and you can select a whole sequence or individual notes.
- Whether to have events beyond the ReClocked Region retain their original positions (Reclock Only within Left and Right Source checked) or retain their time relation to the original material.
- What note divisions are used in the guide sequence (Step Increment).
- The position of the first tempo change (Left Destination). The guide sequence is typically located at the position where the ReClocking begins, but in case it is located elsewhere, you can use this setting to adjust.

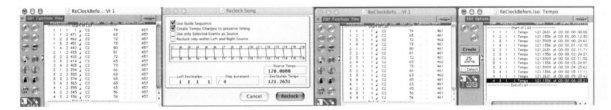

Figure 7.04
Before and after ReClock Song. On the left, irregularly played quarter notes and the ReClock Song setup to align them with tempo changes. On the right, the result – the notes are on the quarter note grid, and there is a tempo change at each quarter note position. Playback sounds the same before and after.

KC Nudge Event Position by …

Beat slicing

If you work with loops, you undoubtedly will want to adjust their tempo and groove to your song at some point. One way is to cut the loop into individual rhythmic events (called slices) and place the individual slices on your audio tracks at the appropriate meter positions. Although software dedicated to that process has more bells and whistles, you can get the job done in Logic.

There are two ways to approach slicing an audio file: by beat and by event. Beat slicing amounts to cutting the audio file into equal-sized pieces whose size corresponds to a standard note duration – typically 8th or 16th notes or perhaps triplets in the case of swing loops. Event slicing amounts to finding individual events, drum hits for example, within the loop and using those as the slice points. Once the loop is sliced and the slices are placed sequentially on an Arrange window track, you can change the tempo and adjust the groove of the slices within reasonable limits.

If your only interest is in adjusting the tempo of the loop, consider the alternative of using one of Logic's time-stretching options. They allow you to adjust an audio Region's length to the nearest bar line or to the cycle length without affecting pitch. Experiment with that process first, trying Logic's five time-stretching algorithms. If the results aren't satisfactory, then try beat or event slicing.

KC   Adjust Object length to Locators
KC   Adjust Object length to nearest bar

Beat slicing is the easiest:

- Open the audio loop in the Sample Editor and ensure it is properly trimmed. If not adjust the end markers to get a perfect loop.
- Drag the audio Region corresponding to the trimmed loop to the desired position in the Arrange window. Set the Left Locator to the beginning of the loop, and set the Right Locator to match the number of bars in the loop.
- Unless Logic's tempo matches that of the loop, the Region length and the Cycle length will be different. You want them to be the same for purposes of beat slicing, but you may not want to mess with the song's tempo, in which case, select an unused tempo alternative.
- Use the Options menu or a key command to change the tempo so that the loop length matches the Cycle length.

M   Options » Tempo » Adjust Tempo using object length & locators
KC   Adjust Tempo using object length & locators.

Figure 7.05
A one bar drum loop is positioned on an Arrange track and Logic's tempo has been set to match the loop's.

- Finally, hold the Option key and use the scissors tool to cut a slice of the size you want at the beginning of the loop. Using the Option key causes Logic to cut the entire loop into equal slices.

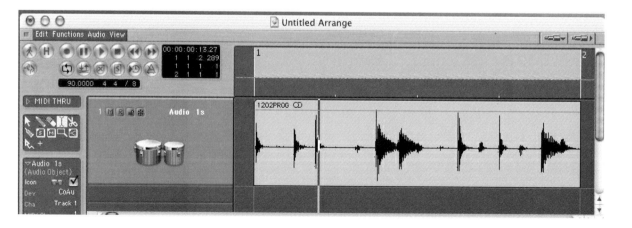

Event slicing starts with the same steps, but instead of using the Scissors tool to create the slices, you need to use Logic's Strip Silence function. That attempts to find individual sonic events by looking for segments of the audio file that exceed a certain threshold.

- With the loop Region selected in the Arrange window, choose Strip Silence from the Arrange window's Audio menu.

Quick tip

Strip Silence can be used in the Audio or Arrange window, but using it in the Arrange window has the advantage that the slices will automatically be placed at their original positions in the loop.

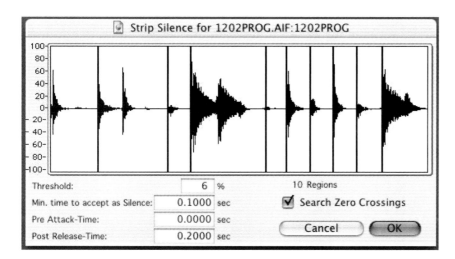

Figure 7.06
The threshold adjustment in the Strip Silence window sets the level below which audio is regarded as silence. Slices are then created to enclose the Regions that are above the threshold (i.e. that are not silent).

- Adjust the threshold setting until you see slices corresponding to individual sonic events. The trick here is to make sure that there aren't any slices that you don't want – too few slices is fine, because you can repeat the process on the resulting Regions to refine the slicing.
- Click 'OK' to slice the loop and automatically place the slices on the Arrange track.
- Select individual slices that contain more than one event, and repeat the Strip Silence process, until each event is its own slice.
- Open a Sample Editor window and ensure it is in Link mode (Link button is pink). Then select each slice in the Arrange window and adjust its start point to the precise beginning of the event in the Sample Editor as needed.
- Close the gaps between slices by selecting all the slices using Logic's Tie Objects by Length Change function.

M   Arrange » Functions » Object » Tie Objects by Length Change.
KC   Tie Objects by Length Change

Quick tip

The Pre-Attack and Post-Release settings adjust the beginning and end of each slice by the indicated time. For beat slicing, use a high release value and a low attack. Usually, you will need to adjust some of the slices in the Arrange window or Sample Editor.

Quick tip

Alternately, you can set a high zoom and use the Scissors tool to create more slices.

Using the slices

Once you have the loop sliced up, you will want to return to the original song tempo. Since the slices are audio Regions, changing the tempo will cause them to either overlap (raising the tempo) or have gaps between them (lowering the tempo). You can adjust for overlaps by decreasing the slice lengths or adding an appropriate fade to each Region.

If you've decreased the tempo and created gaps, you can't adjust by increasing the slice lengths because that will produce double hits. If the gaps are noticeable, you might improve things by adding a little reverb to the track. If that's not satisfactory you'll need to use an event-slicing program like Propellerhead's ReCycle which will pad the gaps for you.

Catching the groove

Once you have the slices, you can turn them into a MIDI groove by creating an empty MIDI sequence, moving the SPL to the beginning of each slice and inserting a MIDI note at each slice position.

KC   Select Next Event
KC   Goto Selection

Entering the notes in a Matrix editor using MIDI step-input is the easiest way to do hat. You might then modify the note pitches in the MIDI sequence to create a bass or lead part or additional percussion that matches the groove of the loop. You can also turn the MIDI file into a groove template for quantizing other sequences.

M   Options » Groove Templates » Make Groove Template.

Figure 7.07
MIDI notes matching the slice positions can be entered by moving the Song Position to the beginning of each slice and adding a note at that position. The notes can then be modified to produce melodies, chords, or other percussion. The MIDI sequence can also be turned into a Groove Template for quantizing other MIDI data.

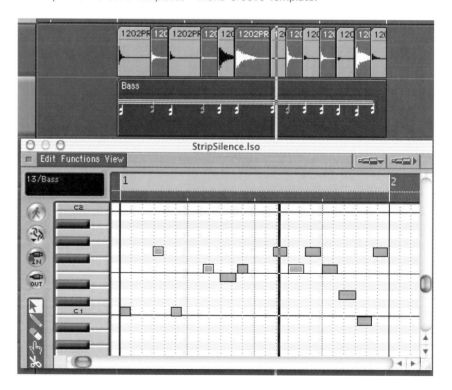

Grooving the catch

Alternatively, you can re-groove the slices to match the groove of your song. If the changes are extreme, you'll have the same gaps and overlaps problem as when changing tempo, but within reasonable limits you can effectively adjust the feel of the loop.

Grooves and Rex files

Rex format files, created by beat-slicing utilities like Propellerhead's Recycle can be imported directly onto audio tracks in Logic or used in the EXS24 sampler. To import a Rex file to an audio track in the Arrange window, Shift-click at the desired location with the Pencil tool or use the Audio menu (in which case the audio Regions will be placed at the SPL).

M   Audio » Import Audio File

Logic will present a file-open dialog followed by an options dialog for importing the Rex file slices. Depending on the song tempo, the slices may overlap and Logic gives you several options for handling that: you can crossfade the slices, you can spread them over additional tracks so that no two slices overlap on the same track, you can merge them into a single audio Region, or you can do nothing and let them overlap.

Once you've imported a Rex file, you can create a MIDI Region matching its groove and turn it into a Groove Template as described above. (See Chapter 8 for more details on using Groove Templates for quantization.)

Quick tip	As an alternative, you could turn the slices, into separate audio files: **Arrange » Audio » Convert Regions to Individual Audio Files**. Those could then be loaded into a sample player and played like any other drum samples.

Info

The point of using slices instead of a single audio Region is that you can then change Logic's tempo and each slice will remain at its original bar/beat position. For a single audio Region, changing the tempo changes the bar/beat position of all audio within the Region.

Quick tip

If you have Emagic's EXS 24 sampler, you can use its Instrument editor to import Rex files as EXS24 Instruments and extract the matching MIDI Region automatically. You'll find those options on the Instrument Editor's **Instrument » Recycle Convert** sub-menu. The options that begin 'Extract sequence…' automatically create matching MIDI files. The ones that begin 'Slice Loop…' simply create an EXS24 Instrument from the Rex file slices. You can later use the same menu to extract the MIDI sequences.

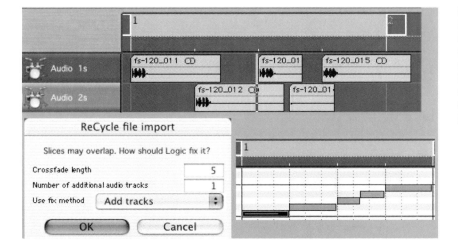

Figure 7.08
Rex file slices can be imported directly to Arrange window tracks (top). The import dialog (lower-left) determines how overlapping Regions will be handled. MIDI Regions reflecting the groove of the slices(lower-right) can be created manually or generated automatically, by importing the Rex file as an EXS24 Instrument.

The MIDI editors

L ogic features four different editors as well as several related windows for entering and processing MIDI data.

- The *Matrix* editor provides a piano-roll style display of MIDI notes. It also has an optional graphic display for other MIDI data. It can show the MIDI data in a single Region or in multiple Regions (with some editing limitations). The Matrix editor is best suited for entering and editing notes graphically.
- The *Score* editor displays MIDI notes using standard music notation. It allows a great deal of freedom in controlling the display without changing the musical data. For example, notes can be 'visually' quantized without affecting their true time position. The Score editor is well suited to note entry and editing for those proficient in music notation.
- The *Event* editor is a list-style display of all MIDI data. Display of individual data types can be toggled on and off. It displays only the data in a single MIDI Region, but can also display a list of all Regions in a Folder as well as all Regions and Folders in the Arrange window. The Event editor is best suited for numerical editing of MIDI data.
- The *Hyper Edit* window is a bar-chart display of all MIDI data. It features separate 'lanes' for each data type and in the case of notes, for each note pitch. The latter makes it useful as a drum editor. It is also the best way to view and edit multiple types of MIDI data, such pan and volume, along the same time line.
- The *Transform* window allows you to select and process all types of MIDI data. It can be used, for example, to convert volume messages to expression messages or to randomize, transpose or otherwise mangle note pitches. This underused feature can become one of your best friends.
- The *Keyboard* window facilitates step entry of MIDI notes into existing Regions. You can step enter notes without it, but using it and its associated key commands greatly enhances the process.
- The *Region Parameters* and Extended Region Parameters windows (a.k.a. Sequence Parameters), though not officially MIDI editors or processors, provide another method of modifying MIDI data in Regions. They are found in the parameters section (left edge) of the Arrange window – the Extended Region Parameters are displayed by double-clicking an empty space in the Region Parameters window.

Quick tip

Both the Transform and Keyboard window should be used in conjunction with one of the MIDI editors to view the results of their action. The Event editor makes a good viewer for the Transform window as do the Matrix or Score editors for the Keyboard window.

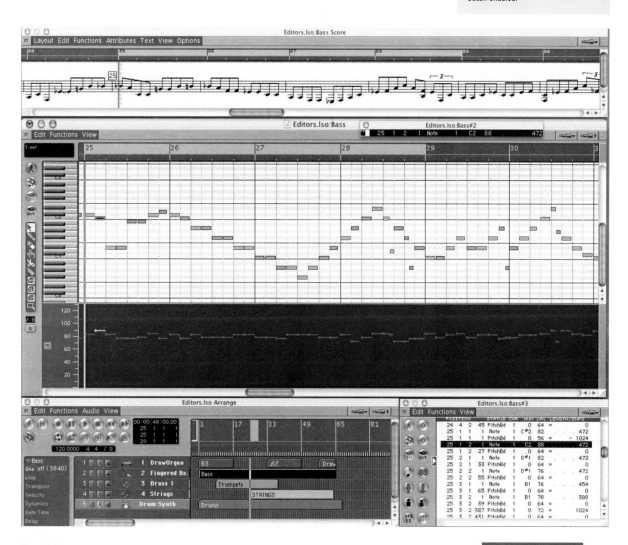

Figure 8.01
Opening several editor windows can be useful when editing. Here a Matrix editor is opened as a standard window (centre) to edit notes and Velocity, while Score editor, Event editor, and Arrange windows are opened as floats and linked to the Matrix editor for display and selection purposes. The Event Float (see below) is also open in the upper-right border of the Matrix editor.

Common editor features

The Functions and Edit menus of all the main editors offer a range of convenient options for selecting and modifying MIDI data.

Handy data editing functions

The Functions menu (see Figure 8.02) offers a number of shortcuts for managing notes. The Note Events sub-menu handles note overlapping, legato, and channelizing for polyphonic voices.

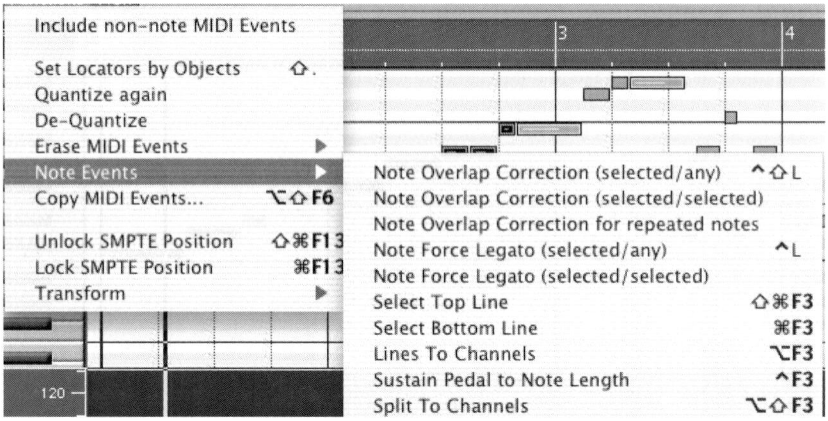

Figure 8.02
The Functions menu has a number of useful options for modifying notes. The Note Events sub-menu (shown here) provides several options for handling overlapping notes and extracting voices from polyphonic parts.

Include non–note MIDI Events	
Set Locators by Objects	⇧.
Quantize again	
De-Quantize	
Erase MIDI Events	▶
Note Events	▶
Copy MIDI Events...	⌥⇧F6
Unlock SMPTE Position	⇧⌘F13
Lock SMPTE Position	⌘F13
Transform	▶

Note Overlap Correction (selected/any)	^⇧L
Note Overlap Correction (selected/selected)	
Note Overlap Correction for repeated notes	
Note Force Legato (selected/any)	^L
Note Force Legato (selected/selected)	
Select Top Line	⇧⌘F3
Select Bottom Line	⌘F3
Lines To Channels	⌥F3
Sustain Pedal to Note Length	^F3
Split To Channels	⌥⇧F3

120 —

Note Overlap Correction shortens notes to ensure that there are at least eight ticks between the end of one note and the start of the next. It can be applied in three modes: selected/any, selected/selected, and repeated notes. Selected/any mode shortens selected notes so they don't overlap any other notes in the Region. Selected/selected mode shortens only notes that overlap other selected notes. Repeated notes mode shortens only notes that overlap other notes of the same pitch.

Note Force Legato both lengthens and shortens notes to ensure that they end exactly eight ticks from the next note. It has two modes: selected/any and selected/selected. Those have the same meaning as for Note Overlap Correction.

Select Top Line, *Select Bottom Line*, and *Lines to Channels* are intended for extracting individual parts from polyphonic Regions. The first two select individual parts and the third separates parts by assigning them different MIDI channels. Demixing by event channel in the Arrange window can then be used to split the parts into separate Regions, if desired.

Copy MIDI events is a powerful dialog for copying and moving MIDI data. You specify a time-range and destination and the number of copies desired then select an operations mode and you're done. Operations modes include merge with existing data at the destination, replace the data at the destination, swap with the data at the destination, or rotate, which moves everything from the end of the range to the destination back towards the beginning of the range.

Handy selection options

The bottom half of the Edit menu offers 13 convenient options for selecting events: *Select All* and *Select All Following*.

KC   Select all *«CO A»*
KC   Deselect all *«SH CO A»*
KC   Select all Following *«SH F»*

•   *Select Inside Locators, Deselect Outside Locators,* and *Toggle Selection*.

KC   Select Inside Locators *«SH I»*
KC   Deselect Outside Locators
KC   Toggle Selection *«SH T»*

•   *Select Empty, Overlapped, Muted,* and *Equal Colored Objects*.

KC   Select empty Objects *«SH U»*
KC   Select Overlapped Objects
KC   Select muted Objects *«SH M»*

•   *Select Equal* and *Similar Objects*.

KC   Select Equal Objects *«SH E»*
KC   Select Similar Objects *«SH S»*

Info

There is no difference between 'Equal' and 'Similar' objects except for MIDI controller messages. All messages for the same controller are similar, but only those with the same value are equal.

•   *Select Equal Channels* and *Subpositions*.

KC   Select Equal Channels *«SH K»*
KC   Select Equal Subpositions *«SH P»*

Info

As mentioned, the position field has four values: Bar, Beat, Division, and Tick. The last three are called the subposition. Selecting equal subpositions, therefore, selects all events at the same position relative to the barlines. That is often confused with equal note divisions. For example, all quarter-notes are not at the same subposition, but the third quarter-note in each bar is at the same subposition.

In addition to the Edit menu options, there are several other handy selection key commands:

•*KC* Select First *«SH Top»* (Top is often labeled 'Home')
•*KC* Select Last *«SH Bottom»* (Bottom is often labeled 'End')
•*KC* Select Previous Event **«Left Arrow»**
•*KC* Select Next Event *«Right Arrow»*
•*KC* Toggle Previous Event *«SH Left Arrow»*
•*KC* Toggle Next Event *«SH Right Arrow»*

Ways to move things around

In Chapter 3, I mentioned moving selected Regions to the SPL using the *Pickup Clock* key command. That also works for selections of MIDI data in any of the editors. There are also key commands – collectively named nudging – for moving selections of events by various increments including: SMPTE frame, half-frame, and

---

Quick tip

The Toggle commands add to the current selection, while the Select commands vacate the current selection.

bit; bar, beat, division (called 'format), and tick. Nudging commands also exist for changing pitch in semitones, changing channel, and changing note length.

- •*KC* Nudge Event Position by ...
- •*KC* Nudge Event Length by ...
- •*KC* Event Transpose ...
- •*KC* Event Channel ...
- •*KC* Nudge Event Position by + Nudge Value *«OP Right Arrow»*
- •*KC* Nudge Event Position by - Nudge Value *«OP Left Arrow»*
- •*KC* Set Nudge Value to ...

MIDI input and output

Each editor window has buttons labelled In and Out in the Parameter area. Respectively, those enable MIDI input for step-entry of data and MIDI output as you select and move data with the mouse. If you want to edit data silently, turn Out off – that won't affect sequence playback or MIDI thru.

The Matrix editor

The Matrix editor is probably Logic's most used editor. It displays notes in a piano-roll style with time running horizontally and pitch, vertically. A piano keyboard at the left indicates pitch. You can open an optional Hyper Draw lane at the bottom of the Matrix editor to display and edit any MIDI event type, including note Velocity.

Figure 8.03
The Matrix editor window with Hyper Draw MIDI pitchbend shown at the bottom. Bars indicate notes. Colours indicate velocity.

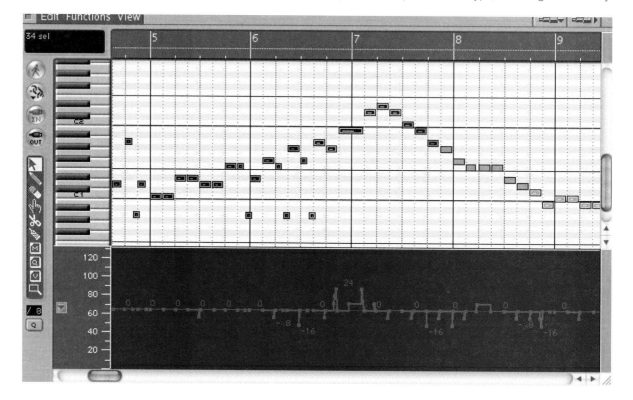

M Windows » Open Matrix Edit
KC Open Matrix Editor *«OP 6»*
•*KC* Toggle Matrix Editor

The Matrix editor can display the MIDI data in one or several Regions. When you open it with no Region selected, it will show the contents of all MIDI Regions on the same level. When you open it with one or more Regions selected, it will show the contents of the last selected Region(s). To go from multiple to single Region display, double-click on any MIDI event in the desired Region. To go from single to multiple Region display, double-click any empty portion of the Matrix window. You can optionally view only the events in selected Regions.

Info

The top left corner of the Matrix editor displays information about the cursor location and the current selection. It shows the cursor location in time and pitch, the number of notes that are selected, and if the notes selected overlap, a guess at the name of the chord formed by the notes.

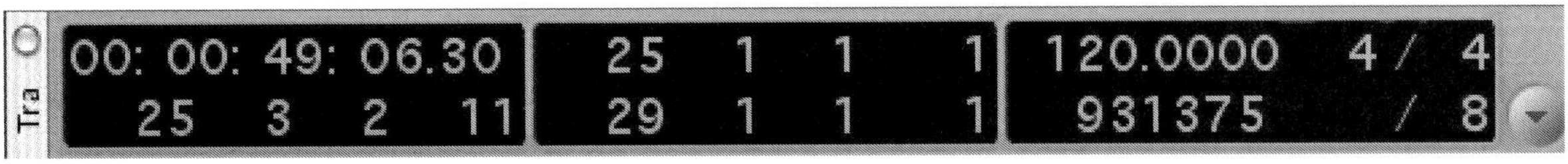

Figure 8.04
A floating Transport window showing only its Position, Locator, and Tempo/Signature displays can be useful when using the Matrix editor.

M Matrix » View » Show Selected Sequences Only

M Matrix » View » Show Sequence Colors

Logic's Division setting affects a number of time-based actions in the Matrix editor. The Division setting is displayed and can be changed in the small window above the Quantize button (with the Q icon). Dragged notes will snap to the Division gridlines, however, if the horizontal zoom is great enough, you can position notes between Division gridlines—snapping will only occur when you get close to a gridline. As mentioned above, you can also nudge selections of notes right or left by one Division using the 'Nudge by Format' key commands. Finally, the Division controls the step size for MIDI step input (see The Keyboard Window on page 86).

Quick tip

Normally Logic uses colour to indicate note Velocity in the Matrix editor, but you can change that behaviour and make note colours match the Region colour. That makes it a lot easier to tell which notes belong to which Regions when multiple Regions are displayed.

Quick tip

When you want to move other MIDI data along with notes in the Matrix editor, use the Functions menu's 'Include non-note MIDI events' option. That causes all MIDI events to be selected in the corresponding area as you make note selections. Then nudging and dragging notes will move those events as well.

You can set the Locators by the selection and start cycle-playback in the Matrix editor just as in the Arrange window. You can also mute selected notes with a key command or the Mute tool (with the M icon). Muted notes are greyed out so they can be easily spotted.

Quick tip

To quickly scroll forward and backward in the Matrix and other time based editor windows (Score in linear mode, Hyper Edit, and Event) use the forward and rewind key commands with Catch enabled.

KC   Mute Objects *«M»*
KC   Select Muted Objects *«SH M»*
•*KC* Forward
•*KC* Rewind
•*KC* Fast Forward «SH ,»
•*KC* Fast Rewind «SH .»

The Score editor

The Score editor is Logic's other note-oriented editor. Musicians proficient at reading music notation tend to prefer the Score editor over the Matrix editor for viewing pitch. On the other hand, the Score editor is not well suited for viewing timing details since notes and note-lengths are visually quantized. If you prefer to work in the Score editor, keeping a linked Matrix or Event editor open as a float provides the best of both worlds.

Figure 8.05
The Score editor window. Notes are displayed in standard music notation.

The Score editor has two viewing modes: linear view (Figure 8.06) and page view (Figure 8.05). The easiest way to switch back and forth is with the Page View button (page icon) at the top of the Score window's parameter area.

M   Score » View » Page Edit
KC   Page Edit

Linear view displays the score along a timeline as in the Matrix editor, and you can open a Hyper Draw lane in Linear view. Page view reflects how the score will appear in print and allows you to view more of the score onscreen. In either view, you can use visual quantizing and intelligent interpretation to display the notes as they would be scored rather than exactly as played.

As with the Matrix editor, you can view a single or multiple Regions in the Score editor, but Score gives you several more ways to control which Regions are displayed.

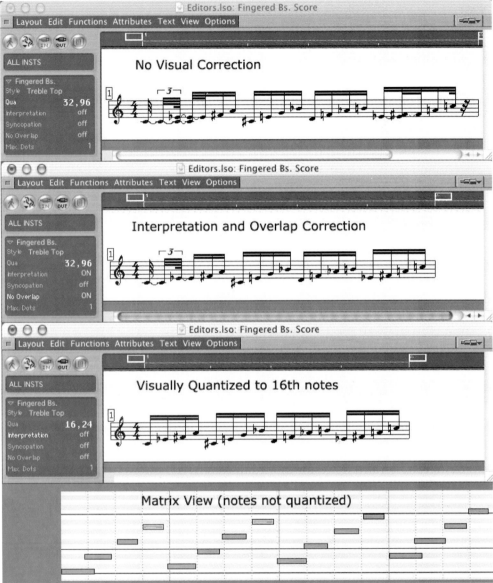

Figure 8.06
Three Scores and a Matrix view of the same notes. With no visual correction (top), the notes appear at their actual time positions, making the score difficult to read. Interpretation and No Overlap (middle) corrects the display of notes that are too long or too short, thereby eliminating some ties. Visual Quantization (bottom) restricts notes to 16th-note positions

- You can set up Instrument sets to show only Regions on tracks assigned to specific Environment objects.
- You can choose whether to display muted tracks, Regions, and individual notes in the Score:Global Format Song Settings.
- You can choose whether to display the contents of Aliases in the Score:Global Format Song Settings. (You can also choose to make them editable.)
- You can turn Score display off for individual Regions and Folders in the Extended Region Parameters.

Quick tip

Keep in mind that loops are never displayed in any of the MIDI editors and Aliases can only be displayed in the Score editor.

Figure 8.07
The Score editor's Part Box has 16 sections (top left), each of which can be detached as a floating window (right) by double-clicking the section icon in the Part Box. The select section's parts are also displayed below the Part Box (bottom left). Finally, click-holding the section-icon will reveal a drop-down menu showing the parts. Parts can be dragged into the score from any of those locations.

The Part Boxes

The Score editor's 16 Part Boxes are represented by icons just below the Toolbox. Double-click an icon to open the Part Box as a floating window. Click-hold the icon to open the Part Box as a drop-down menu. Click the icon to bring the Part Box to the top of the window below the icons, which displays all the Part Boxes simultaneously. You can drag symbols from any of those Part Box views into the score.

Part Boxes are provided for notes, rests, key and time signatures, bar lines, dynamics markings and other score symbols, tempo markers, and text entry. Text entry has separate modes for text, lyrics, chords, and song data such as instrument, date, song name, etc.

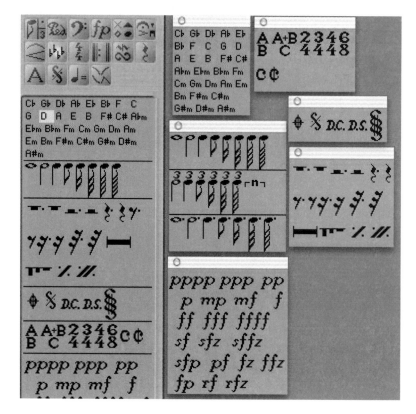

Time and key signature changes

You can change the time and key signature at any measure in the score by dragging the associated symbol from the Part Box into the score. Time signature changes are also indicated in the Bar Ruler, whereas key signature changes are only shown in the score. The Transport's Tempo/Signature section also always displays the time signature at the SPL location.

Time and key signature changes are actually managed in a separate, list-editor like window called the Signature/Key Change List Editor which can be opened from the Global Options menu. You can copy, paste, delete, and move both types of events from that window.

KC Signature/Key Change List Editor... *«CO O»*

The Event editor

The Event editor allows you to view and edit all MIDI data in a time-sorted list. You can choose to view some or all MIDI data types using the buttons on the left. The bottom-right button, with the 0's and 1's icon, toggles display of extra lines of data

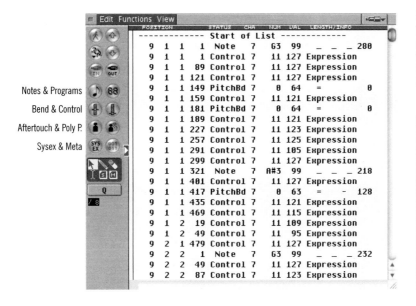

Notes & Programs

Bend & Control

Aftertouch & Poly P.

Sysex & Meta

Figure 8.08
The Event editor window. All MIDI data is shown in a list. Buttons at the left allow you to suppress individual MIDI data types. The Position display's four digits represent: Bars, Beats, Divisions, and Ticks.

Quick tip

The Event editor shows the contents of one MIDI Region at a time, but it can also be used to show a sorted list of all Regions and Folders in the Arrange window or within any Folder. In that view, both audio and MIDI Regions are shown. That is often a convenient alternative to the Arrange window for selecting Regions for editing in other Content-Linked windows.

for SysEx (which is not limited in length) and note events, for which note-off Velocity is shown. If you Command-click one of the buttons, a new event of that type will be created.

The Event editor's View menu allows you to choose among several convenient viewing modes. You can view time values (position and length) in SMPTE units instead of the default bars, beats, divisions, and ticks. You can show note lengths as the position of the end of the note, which is handy for gauging whether notes are overlapping. You can view positions relative to the beginning of the Region (called 'Local') rather than to the beginning of the song. Finally, you can view SysEx data values in hexadecimal notation rather than decimal, which is the format most often used in synthesizer operations manuals.

Quick tip

You can select multiple events for editing, but if they are not all of the same type, some parameters won't be changeable. For those parameters that you can change, changes will be relative for all selected events. If you want to change all events to the same value, hold the Option key while making the change.

Quick tip

If you want to edit event data numerically while working in other editors, consider opening the Event Float, which displays just the selected event.

M Options » Event Float…
KC Toggle Event Float «OP E»

Figure 8.09
You can use the Event Float to edit selected MIDI events numerically or by scrolling. Click its disk icon at the left to change the time display from Bars/Beats to SMPTE. Command-click the disk icon to suppress MIDI output when scrolling values (which can be annoying when adjusting note Velocity, for example).

The Hyper editor

Perhaps because of its special features, Logic's Hyper Edit window is underused. It provides a time-synchronized, bar-chart style display using different *lanes* to display different types of MIDI data. The bar height indicates note Velocity for MIDI notes and indicates the data value for all other MIDI data. The Hyper Edit window is the easiest way to view and edit several kinds of MIDI data at once. It also makes a great drum-track editor because you can set up a lane for each drum sound (i.e. pitch) as in Figure 8.10.

Figure 8.10
The Hyper Edit window. Each event type including individual note pitches has its own bar-chart lane. Here six individual drum parts are shown.

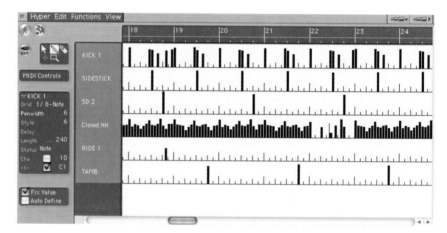

Each lane in the Hyper editor has its own set of display parameters, called a Hyper Definition. You can create Hyper Sets containing any combination of Hyper Definitions, meaning you can completely customize what is displayed in the Hyper editor as well as how it is viewed. The drop-down menu just below the Toolbox allows you to select from among the Hyper Sets you've created, and a number of convenient ones have been set up for you.

The Hyper editor's Hyper menu provides options for conveniently setting up your own Hyper Sets. Here are some examples:

• Use Create Hyper Set to create a new Hyper Set with a single lane for MIDI Volume. If you don't want to show MIDI Volume, select that lane and choose 'Delete Event Definition' from the Hyper menu. You'll now have an empty Hyper Set.

- In an Event editor, select at least one event of each type you want to include in a Hyper Set then choose 'Multi Create Event Definition' from the Hyper menu. Lanes for each selected event type will be added to the current Hyper Set.
- Select all events in a Region and choose 'Create Hyper Set for Current Events'. Lanes will be created for only the MIDI Control Change events selected.

Each Hyper Definition has its own set of display parameters that control what is displayed, how it appears, and how new events are added with the Pencil tool.

Grid: Determines both the display grid and the selection resolution. When you select an event, all events within the same grid division are selected.
Penwidth: Sets the width of the bars.
Style: Sets the style of the bars. Six styles are offered, the last three of which flash to indicate selected events.

Quick tip

The function of the Grid in the Hyper Editor takes some getting used to, and you will probably find yourself modifying multiple events unintentionally until you become accustomed to it. The trick is to set a very high resolution (small Grid size) when editing. Large Grid sizes can be very convenient when you're creating events – it is similar to the snap-quantize feature found in other software.

Delay: Shifts events by a positive or negative number of ticks. The Delay setting also applies to newly entered events.
Length: Sets the length of notes added with the Pencil tool. (Notice that there is no visual indication of note length or way of editing it after the fact in the Hyper Editor.)
Status: Selects the type of MIDI event viewed and edited.
Cha: When checked, only events on the selected MIDI channel will be displayed.
-1-: When checked, only events with the specified first data byte will be displayed. This setting applies only to notes, Poly Pressure, and Control Change messages. For notes and Poly Pressure it represents pitch and for Control Change messages it represents the MIDI controller number.

Quick tip

To move or copy selected events, hold the Shift key and click any selected event. Events can be moved to different positions in the same lane as well as to different lanes. When moved to different lanes, they will automatically be converted to that lane's Hyper Definition. That's a very convenient way to audition the effect of moving a drum part from one drum sound to another. Use the Option key with the Shift key to copy instead of move.

Info

The Hyper Editor displays MIDI data from one Region at a time. You can think of a Hyper Set as a display template or setup, but don't confuse it with the actual data displayed. Any Hyper Set can be used to view the data in any MIDI Region.

Quick tip

Hold the Shift key when selecting events with the Selection tool either individually or by rubber-banding. Otherwise, the touched events (and all other events within the same Grid division) will be altered in value.

Quick tip

The Fix Value checkbox can save you a world of grief when using the Hyper Editor. When checked, values will not be altered by either the Selection or Pencil tool. (No accidental drag-modifying while trying to select or enter data.) When Fix Value is activated, new events created with the Pencil tool will take the value of the most recently selected event.

KC   Protect Values toggle.

Quick tip

The Auto Define checkbox will cause Hyper Definitions to be automatically created as you select events in any other editor. That's a great way to quickly create a custom Hyper Set, but don't forget to turn it off when you're finished.

KC   Auto Define toggle *«CT A»*

Transform window tips

Logic's Transform window is another underused asset. Once you make friends with it you'll wonder how you got by without it. You can use it to select, move, and modify any kind of MIDI data and it can be applied within a single Region or across many Regions at the same time.

Figure 8.11
The Transform window allows you to select and modify MIDI events in one or more Regions. Here notes have their position and velocity offset by a small, random amount to humanize the feel.

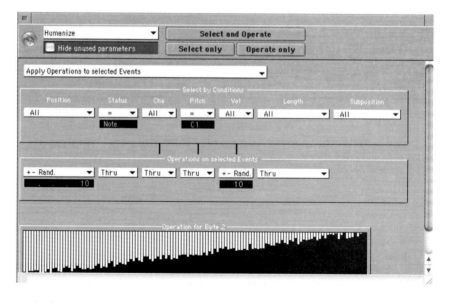

Quick tip

As with Logic's other windows, the Transform window's Link button (upper left) will link its range of application to selections in other windows (see Chapter 2 for details). It is a good idea to keep this in Link (pink) or Contents Link (yellow) mode to ensure that you don't make unwanted Transformations. If you're selecting Regions in the Arrange or Event editor window, Contents Link mode is a good choice. If you're selecting events in one of the MIDI editors, Link mode is a good choice. The label at the top of the Transform window always shows the current target of its actions.

At the top left of the Transform window there is a drop-down menu of Transform Sets. By default there are a number of useful factory Transform Sets, and you can of course, create your own. Two things to keep in mind are that any changes you make automatically become part of the current Transform Set, and Transform Sets are saved with each song (i.e. they are not Global). You can, however, import another song's Transform Sets using the File menu's Import Settings dialog.

The centre portion of the Transform window is divided into two sections labeled 'Select by Conditions' (Conditions for short) and 'Operations on selected Events' (Operations for short). (The fourth and fifth Conditions will be labelled –1- and –2- unless the Status Condition is set to Notes, in which case they will be labeled Pitch and Velocity.)

Three buttons at the top and a drop-down menu just above the Conditions, control how the Conditions and Operations are applied. The buttons allow you to Select only (i.e. only apply the Conditions), Operate only (i.e. only apply the Operations), or Select and Operate (i.e. apply the Conditions then Operate on the resulting selection.)

The drop-down menu further modifies the Transform window's behaviour when the Operations are performed. (It has no effect when only the Conditions are applied.) Three of the options apply the Operations in different ways, while the fourth, Delete selected Events, does just what you would expect. The Operations can be simply applied to the selected events, applied to the selected events while deleting unselected events, or applied to copies of the selected events.

Quick tip

To extract one type of MIDI data from a Region, first make a copy of the Region. Open the Transform window and put it in Content Link mode by clicking the Link button until it is yellow. Set the Conditions to select the data type you want to extract and leave the Operations blank. Select the original Region, use Delete Selected mode and click the Select and Operate button. Select the copy of the Region, use the Apply Operations and Delete unselected Events mode, and click the Select and Operate button again. The copied Region now contains the extracted data and the original Region contains everything else.

Quick tip

There is no way to delete Transform Sets once they are created. This longstanding design oversight makes it possible to create large, unwieldy Transform Set menus, so create new ones sparingly.

Quick tip

Selections can be extended by holding down the Shift key while clicking the Select only or Select and Operate buttons. That allows you to change Conditions several times to include different data, then operate on the combined selection. For example, you could use multiple Subposition Conditions to select all even-numbered eighth-notes, then modify their position and Velocity to create a customized swing.

The three vertical bars between the Conditions and Operations sections are called *Swap Bars*. They only affect Operations and as their name implies, they move data to different positions in MIDI messages. (Most MIDI messages consist of three bytes, the first signals the message type as well as the channel number and the last two carry data values.) For example, you can move the channel number to the first or second data position or swap the first and second data positions. For notes the first and second data positions are pitch and velocity, respectively. For MIDI Control Change messages they are the controller number and value. As an example of how to use Swap Bars, here are the steps to make MIDI panning track note pitch.

- Set the Status Condition to select Notes. Leave the remaining Conditions set to All.
- Set the Status Operation to Control. Set the Pitch Operation to Fix with a value of 10. (Pan is MIDI controller number 10.)
- Click the Velocity Swap Bar so that it links the Pitch Condition to the Velocity Operation.
- Set the Operations mode to Copy Selected events Apply Operation.
- Click the Select and Operate button.
- Open the Region in the Event editor. You will see two MIDI pan events following each MIDI note event. Select one of the pan events with value 0, then use the Edit menu to select equal objects and delete them. Those resulted from the MIDI note-off messages, but you don't want to reset the pan to far left at each time a note is released.

- Select one of the remaining pan events and use the Edit menu to select similar objects. The rest of the pan events should now be selected. Click on the last position field (ticks) and scroll down a few ticks. That places the new pan events before the note event that created them. Some synths do not pan notes that are already sounding, and this will ensure the pan messages come first.

If you set the -2- (a.k.a. velocity) Operation to anything other than Thru, you will notice a graphic appear at the bottom of the Transform window. That is called the Universal Map and it has many uses. If you choose any Operation other than Use Map, it will simply display the result of the Operation for all 128 MIDI data values. If you select Use Map, or set one of the Conditions to Map, you will be able to set your own values either graphically or using the numericals at its lower left. That allows you to define your own numerical Operations and Conditions, starting with the displayed values.

Quick tip

Using Map as a Condition can be a little tricky at first. When you do so, two numericals appear for you to set the Condition range. Every incoming event is then examined to see if its data value **is mapped** to a value within that range. If for example, you set the Status Condition to 'Control' and set the -1- Condition to Map with both range values set to 0, only those MIDI control messages for which the Map has a value of 0 for their controller number will be affected. To select just pan messages, for example, ensure the Map has visible bars (i.e. not value 0) everywhere except at position 10 and ensure position 10 has value 0.

Figure 8.12

The Keyboard window is for step-entering MIDI data. You can use the onscreen keyboard or a MIDI controller. Buttons on the left select step size. Buttons on the right select velocity when the onscreen keyboard is used.

The Keyboard window

Logic's Keyboard window is a recent addition to facilitate step-entry of MIDI notes. It can be used in conjunction with any of Logic's MIDI editors to add notes to any MIDI Region. (If no MIDI editor is open, it has no effect.) MIDI step entry of notes

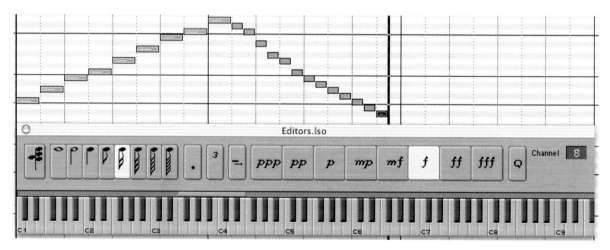

is still possible without opening the Keyboard window, but the Keyboard window offers both visual and functional advantages whether you use MIDI or its onscreen keys to enter notes.

Quick tip

Each MIDI editor has a button labelled 'In' to activate MIDI step input. You don't need to turn this on if you're entering notes from the onscreen keyboard, but you do need to activate it for MIDI step entry, whether the Keyboard window is open or not.

Quick tip

The note-value, triplet, dotted, and quantize buttons also affect MIDI step input.

The buttons above the keyboard graphic are for selecting note value (whole note to 128th note) and Velocity (16 to 127 in steps of 16). The multi-note button on the left will cause clicked notes to be recorded at the same time position (i.e. to create chords) as long as it is on (white background). The buttons with the '3' and '•' icons are for entering triplets and dotted notes. Triplet mode turns off automatically after three notes are entered, and dotted mode turns off automatically after two notes are entered. The Quantize button ('Q' icon) at the right end of the keyboard forces step entry to start at the closest position corresponding to the selected note value.

There are key commands for each of the Keyboard window's buttons as well as for note pitch and octave. When the Keyboard window is not open, the keys assigned to those commands are freed up for other uses.

Extended Region Parameters

The Region Parameters and Extended Region Parameters boxes at the top of the Arrange window's Parameter area provide non-destructive modification of pitch,

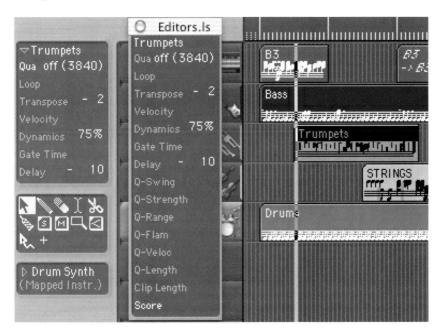

Figure 8.13
Region Parameters (left) and Extended Region Parameters allow you to modify various note parameters for single or multiple Regions. The effects are non-destructive unless 'fixed' using a menu selection.

velocity, dynamics, MIDI delay, note length, and various quantize parameters. They can be set for multiple Regions at once and changing them will cause relative changes for each affected Region. To set a parameter to the same value for all selected Regions, change it while holding the option key. The Arrange window's Functions menu has options for making these non-destructive values permanent.

M   Arrange » Functions » Sequence Parameter » Normalize Sequence Parameters
M   Arrange » Functions » Sequence Parameter » Normalize w/o Channel
M   Arrange » Functions » Sequence Parameter » Normalize w/o Channel & Delay
M   Arrange » Functions » Sequence Parameter » Fix Quantize

Quantizing

All the editors allow you to quantize selected MIDI events using standard note values or any Groove Template you've created (see page 89). Although the Quantize drop-down menu (button with Q icon) only specifies the quantize amount, you can also apply the Extended Region Parameters quantize options. As you change any of the Q parameters, you will see the effect in the Matrix editor.

Quick tip

You can open the Extended Region Parameters for the selected Region by double-clicking in an empty area of the Region Parameters box at the top of the Arrange window's parameter area. Once open, it can be dragged to a convenient position in or near the editor window. It will always display the current quantize setting as well as various quantize parameters, all of which apply as individual notes are quantized.

•*KC* Quantize Again
•*KC* Quantize: next value
•*KC* Quantize: previous Value
•*KC* De-Quantize

The effect of quantizing is influenced by six settings in the Extended Region Parameters:

Q-Swing: Moves even numbered points in the quantization grid either earlier or later in time. Range is 1% to 99%. Default is 50% (unaltered).
Q-Strength: How much each note is quantized towards the closest quantization grid point. 0% for none, 100% for snap to the grid.
Q-Range: The distance in ticks from the closest quantize grid point beyond which Logic will leave notes unquantized.
Q-Flam: Chords (groups of notes starting at exactly the same time) are arpeggiated up (positive values) or down (negative values) by this number of ticks.
Q-Velocity: Controls how much note Velocity is affected by the velocity of the notes in a Groove Template.
Q-Length: Controls how much note length is affected by the lengths of the notes in a Groove Template.

Info

Logic uses a process called Linear Quantize, which attempts to preserve the feel of the original recording while tightening up the timing. With Q-Strength settings of less than 100%, notes farther from the closest quantize grid point are moved more than notes closer to their grid points.

Quick tip

If you enter a negative Q-Range value, Logic will not quantize notes within that distance, but will quantize those farther away. Thus only notes way out of line will be quantized.

Groove Templates

Groove Templates provide an alternative to quantizing to a note-value grid. The positions of the notes in the Groove Template are used to create a quantize grid. You can make any MIDI Region a Groove Template by selecting it and using the menu selection or key command.

M   Options » Groove Templates » Make Groove Template
KC   Make Groove Template

One or two measure, monophonic Regions with regularly spaced notes (for example, a ride cymbal playing 16th notes) make the most useful templates. You can remove a Groove Template by selecting the Region used to make it and using the menu selection or key command.

M   Options » Groove Templates » Remove Groove Template from List
KC   Remove Groove Template from List

Quick tip

See Chapter 7 for tips on extracting Groove Templates from audio Regions and Rex files.

Working with audio files

Audio files can be opened in either the Arrange window or the Audio window. In the Arrange window, Shift-click the desired location with the Pencil tool. In the Audio window choose Add Audio File from Audio File menu. In either case, an Open File dialog will appear allowing you to choose the audio file to open.

M Audio » Audio File » Add Audio File
KC Add Audio File *«CT F»*

Info

The most important thing to understand about working with audio in Logic is the distinction between audio files and audio Regions. Audio files are data files on your hard drive, whereas audio Regions are references to segments of those audio files. Each audio file can have many Regions, and they can be overlapping or separate. Different Regions can even represent exactly the same segment of the audio file, which is what happens when you drag-copy a Region in the Arrange window.

Quick tip

You can save individual Regions as new audio files using the Audio window's Audio File menu as well as by using a key command in the Arrange window.

Regions are part of the Logic song file, not part of the file on your hard drive. If you've created Regions in one song and open the same audio file in another song, the Regions will not be there. But, if you copy/paste an audio file from one song to another, the Regions will be preserved.

M Audio » Audio File » Save Region(s) As…
KC Convert Regions to Individual Audio Files *«CT F»*

The Audio window

Audio files in the Audio window are represented as drop-down lists of audio Regions from those files. When you open an audio file in Logic, whether you do it from the Arrange window or the Audio window, it is placed at the end of the audio file list in the Audio window and a Region encompassing the entire file is created automatically.

KC Show All Regions *«CT Down Arrow»*
KC Hide All Regions *«CT Up Arrow»*

You can resize audio Regions from either end, in both the Audio and Arrange windows. You can also reposition the Region's Anchor in the Audio window. However,

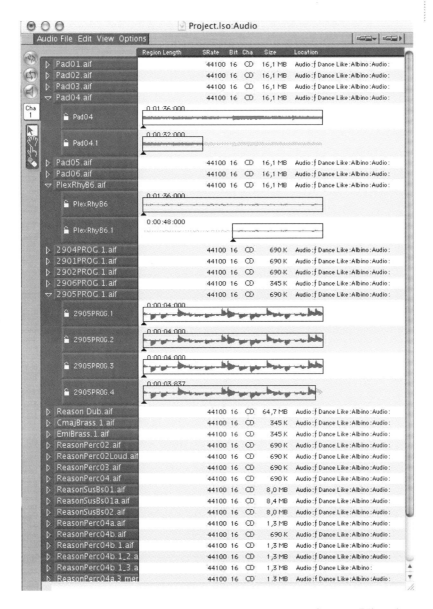

Figure 9.01
Logic's Audio window represents audio files from your hard drive as drop-down lists of audio Regions, which refer to segments of those files. When you open an audio file in either the Arrange window or Audio window, a Region encompassing the entire file is automatically created.

Quick tip

You can sort the Audio window's file list from its View menu by name, size, location on your hard drive, or bit depth. Choosing 'none' from the sort menu will return the list to the order in which the files were opened.

for detailed adjusting of audio Regions and Anchors, the Sample Editor (see Chapter 10) is a better choice.

Info

Once a Region has been placed in the Arrange window, Logic will attempt to preserve the time position of the Anchor. If you move the Anchor in the Audio window, all occurrences of the Region in the Arrange window will adjust to keep their Anchors at their original time positions. Similarly, if you adjust the left boundary by an amount that does not interfere with the Anchor, the Anchor will remain at the same time position. If you drag the left boundary past the Anchor, the Anchor will become attached to the left boundary and will thereafter move. (You can't drag the right boundary past the Anchor.)

Quick tip

In addition to a beginning and end, each audio Region has an Anchor, which is used to position the Region in the Arrange window. When you drag a Region from the Audio window to the Arrange window, it is the Anchor that is placed at the drop point when you release the mouse button.

The Audio window's Audio File menu provides a number of file and Region management functions. You can create new Regions; delete, backup, copy, and move files; change a file's format, and optimize files by deleting portions that are not used in the song. The last operation frees up hard drive space, but can also delete data you use or want to use in another song.

KC   Select Previous Audio File *«Arrow Up»*
KC   Select Next Audio File *«Arrow Down»*
KC   Play/Stop Region *«Space»*

Quick tip

You can assign the same keys to the Arrange and Audio windows' key commands for stepping through tracks (Arrange) and Regions (Audio) as well as for Play/Stop. The active window will determine which action takes place. These are assigned the same keys by default.

Quick tip

Audio Regions have a tendency to proliferate as you work with them in the Arrange window and the Sample editor. You can quickly find which Regions are actually used in your song with the Select Used/Unused menu options and key commands. Periodically deleting unused regions improves Audio window organization and conserves screen real estate.

M   Audio » Edit » Select Used/Unused
KC   Select Used
KC   Select Unused *«SH U»*

Playback from the Audio window

You can play back Regions directly from the Audio window by click-holding in a Region display at the position you want playback to start, or by clicking the Play button (speaker icon) on the left side of the Audio window. You can also initiate playback using key commands, and for consistency, it's a good idea to use the same key assignments you use in the Arrange window.

KC Play/Stop Region *«Space»*

Arranging Audio Regions

The easiest way to get a new Region into your arrangement is to drag it to the desired location (track and time) in the Arrange window. But you only need to do

Quick tip

Option-dragging creates a new Region for the same segment of the audio file. That's similar to making a copy of a MIDI Region. Changes to the Regions' boundaries and Anchors can be made independently. Shift-Option dragging creates a copy of the same Region. That's like creating an Alias of a MIDI file. Changes to a Region's boundaries or Anchor apply to all copies. Keep in mind that any destructive edits to the audio file itself will affect all Regions referring to the file.

that the first time you use a Region – thereafter you can Option-drag or Shift-Option-drag in the Arrange window to create new Regions or copies of Regions at other locations.

Figure 9.02
Once placed in the Arrange window, audio Regions can be copied, aliased or looped just like MIDI Regions. They can also be packed into folders for organizational or complex looping purposes.

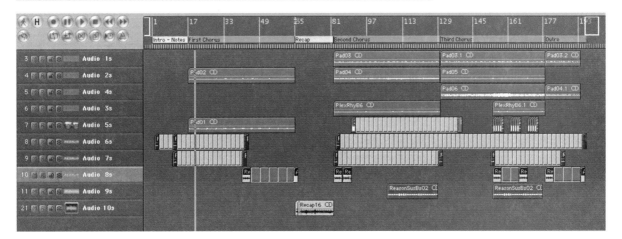

Audio Regions can be looped just like MIDI Regions, but there are some differences:

- Using the menu selections to turn loops to Aliases or real copies have the same effect. Both produce copies of the Region—no new Regions are created.
- If you loop an audio Region contained in a Folder, playback will not stop at the end of the Folder, as it does with MIDI Regions.

Fades and crossfades

Although you can assign several Arrange tracks to the same Environment Audio object, you can only use those tracks to play one Region at a time. On the other hand, you can overlap Regions on the same Arrange track, then use Logic's cross-fade feature to smoothly transition from one to the other.

Figure 9.03
Three methods of dealing with overlapping audio Regions: let playback overlap on different tracks (top), fade one out while the other fades in on a different track (middle), or crossfade between them on a single track (bottom). The fade-in/fade-out method allows slightly greater flexibility in the crossfade curve at the cost of using an additional audio track.

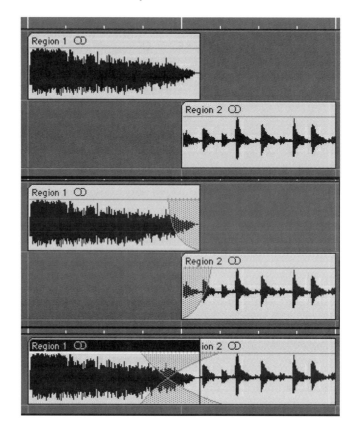

You can create fade ins, fade outs, and crossfades graphically with the Arrange window's crossfade tool ('<' icon) or numerically in the audio Region's Parameter Box. When you use the crossfade tool, click-dragging changes the crossfade length – hold the Control key to change the shape of the curve.

Info

Fades are automatically updated whenever you start playback, but they are not updated in real time as playback proceeds. All crossfades are automatically stored in a separate crossfade file in the same folder as the song. It has the same name as the song followed by – f16 or – f24 depending on the sampling rate. The fade definitions are also saved with the song, so if you accidentally delete the fade file, it will be recreated automatically and you won't loose your fades. (Don't delete the fade file while the song is open!)

Quick tip

Creating fades within a Folder and looping or Aliasing the Folder is the easiest way to repeat complex fades.

When you combine Regions into a single audio file using Logic's Digital Mixdown, Bounce, or Freeze operations, all fades will be preserved in the resulting audio file. In the case of overlapping Regions on the same track where a crossfade has not been created, Logic will use a short default crossfade, for which you can set the time and shape in the Crossfade Options dialog.

M   Arrange » Audio » Digital Mixdown
KC   Merge Objects / Digital Mixdown *«-30»* (] separate key)
M   Arrange » Audio » Default Audio Crossfade Options
KC   Audio Crossfade Options for Merge *«OP +»*

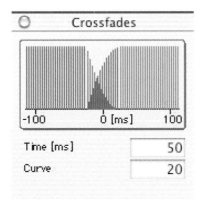

Figure 9.04
The Audio Crossfade Options dialog allows you to set up a default crossfade time and curve, which Logic will use when bouncing or mixing down overlapping audio Regions. If you've created a crossfade graphically on the Region, that will be used instead.

Bouncing

You can use Logic's Bounce operation to create mixes combining your audio tracks into one or several audio files.

There are two Bounce modes:

- Realtime bouncing renders the output to a new audio file as it plays back. Incoming MIDI is processed and incoming audio routed to the bounced output is rendered. That's the method to use when you want to include the audio from external MIDI devices and when you want to include real-time automation using a hardware control surface.
- Offline bouncing processes everything on the included tracks as fast as your CPU can handle it. That will be faster than real time if real-time playback doesn't push your CPU to the limit, and it will be slower if your CPU can't actually process all the data in real time. External audio and MIDI input is ignored.

When you click an Audio Output's Bounce button, a dialog opens allowing you to set up the bounce parameters. Set a start and end position, which by default will be set to the Left and Right Locator positions. Choose a file format – AIFF, SDII, WAVE, and MP3 are supported. Choose file bit-depth resolution (8, 16, or 24 bit) and dithering options. Specify Offline or Realtime. If you want to use the bounced audio in the song, click the Bounce & Add button. Otherwise, click the Bounce button. You will be prompted for a location for the bounced audio file, then Logic will proceed with the bounce.

Quick tip

The Bounce operation is invoked using the Bounce button found on the channel strip for any Audio Output object. That's your tip-off that what gets bounced is the audio from a single Audio Output object. Audio routed to a different output and audio from muted tracks or Regions does not get bounced. All effects processing that appears at the bounced output does get bounced. *In short, what you hear from that output is what you get.*

Quick tip

When Offline bouncing is faster than real time, it is a great way to quickly find the max level for plug-in effects that feature level monitoring. Use it, for example, to set the Input Scaling for the Ad-Limiter plug-in.

Figure 9.05
Logic's Bounce operation will render audio track and plug-in instrument playback to audio files in various formats and bit-depths. You can even use it to encode MP3 files.

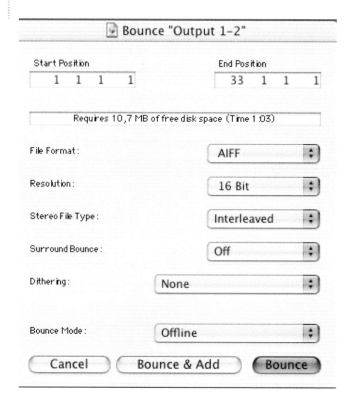

Figure 9.05
Logic's Bounce operation will render audio track and plug-in instrument playback to audio files in various formats and bit-depths. You can even use it to encode MP3 files.

Quick tip

Bouncing normally produces a single stereo or mono file, or split stereo files. If you want separate audio files created for multiple tracks or audio-instrument plug-ins, you can use the Surround Bounce option (see Chapter 11). For that to work, the Audio Objects for the bounced tracks need to be routed and panned to outputs matching the Surround Preferences settings.

Freezing

Freezing is a variation of bouncing intended for reducing the load on your CPU, thereby allowing you to use more tracks and plug-ins than your CPU can handle in one gulp. You invoke Freezing for audio tracks and audio plug-in instruments using the Freeze button (snowflake icon) in the Arrange window's Track List. (If the Freeze buttons are not visible, use the View menu to make them so.)

Freezing is completely managed by Logic and produces separate, temporary, 32-bit audio files for each frozen track. Logic then plays those files instead of processing the data and plug-ins on the frozen tracks. You can unFreeze individual tracks as needed to make necessary modifications.

Freezing is invoked automatically when you initiate playback when the Freeze status of any track has been changed. Alternately, you can initiate Freezing from the global Audio menu or with a key command. In either case, an Offline bounce is performed from the beginning to the end of the song. At the end of the process, Logic does not start playing—you need to hit play again to initiate playback.

M   Audio » Refresh Freeze Files
KC   Refresh Freeze Files *«F»*

Audio housekeeping

When you have a more-or-less final arrangement of a song, here are some steps to organize and optimize its audio files and audio instruments.

- Save the song under a different name and perform these operations on the new song. That allows you to always return to the original song if need be.
- (Optional) Separately bounce Audio Instrument plug-in tracks that will need no further editing, then replace them with audio tracks playing the bounced files.
- (Optional) Separately bounce each MIDI instrument track to a separate file, then replace them with audio tracks playing the bounced files. (Same reasoning as above.)

Quick tip

Audio instruments tend to require a lot of CPU and may not be available if you transfer the song to another computer for mixdown. They also may not be available if you need to remix the song in the distant future. The closer you can get to a song containing only audio tracks, the better.

- (Optional) Separately bounce audio tracks using plug-ins that will not need further editing, then replace them with audio tracks playing the bounced files. (Same reasoning as above.)
- Select unused Regions and delete them.
- If you use the Logic's Project Manager (see Chapter 13), use its Consolidate Selected Songs option to create a self-contained version of the song, its audio files, and remaining plug-in settings. If you do not use the Project Manager, continue with the steps below.
- From the Audio window, copy all files that you may use again in other songs or applications, to a separate folder with a name similar to the song name. Use the option of replacing the files in the song with their copies.
- From the Audio window, move all files that you will not use again, to the same folder.
- Select all files in the Audio window and optimize.

Quick tip

You can change the Freeze file bit depth in the Audio Preferences. If you want to import Freeze files manually into another Logic song (for example on a different computer that doesn't have some of the plug-ins originally used), change it to 24 bits, because Logic doesn't support 32-bit audio files.

Quick tip

If you don't want the Freeze process to continue to the end of the song, you can abort it at any point with Command-Period. That can greatly speed things up when you're Freezing a short track in a long song. Freezing always starts from the beginning of the song, however.

Quick tip

When you've completed the above steps, make a backup of your song or project and all related files.

The Sample editor

10

Figure 10.01
Audio files can be viewed in the Sample editor by double-clicking them in either the Audio or Arrange window. The Bar Ruler at the top of the Sample editor measures relative to start of the audio file when Regions are opened from the Audio window. It measures from the start of the song when Regions are opened from the Arrange window.

L ogic's Sample editor window is primarily for destructive editing of audio files, but it is also a good place to create and fine tune Regions. Audio files can be opened in the Sample editor by double-clicking any audio Region in either the Arrange or Audio window. (You can also use a key command or the Audio menu.) In Link mode, the Sample editor will automatically update to show the selected Region.

M Audio » Sample Editor
KC Open Sample Editor

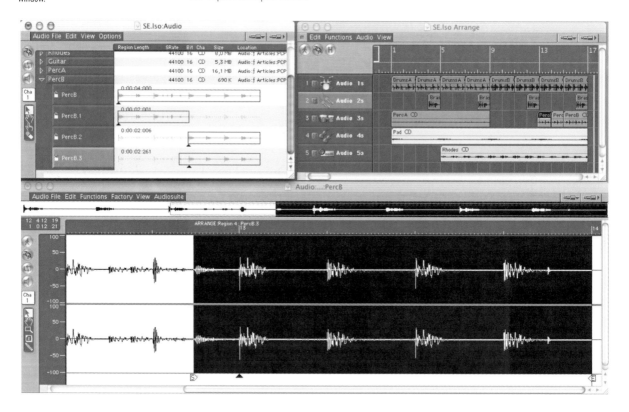

The Sample Editor always shows a single Region within the context of its parent audio file. That allows you to easily adjust Region boundaries and Anchors, to move the Region to other parts of the audio file, and to create new Regions from your actions.

The top-left corner of the Bar Ruler shows the source of the Region being viewed. As a further guide, the division lines are dashed if the Region was opened from the Audio window and are solid if it was opened from the Arrange window.

As mentioned in Chapter 9, Regions are characterized by three locations within an audio file: their start, end, and Anchor. Movable tabs at the bottom of the Sample editor (see Figure10.01) display and allow you to set those locations.

The Start and End tabs are rectangles with a wedge on one side. The point where the wedge joins the rectangle indicates the exact position of the tab.

The display at the top-left of the Sample Editor, which normally shows start point (top) and length (bottom) of the selection, changes temporarily while the Anchor is being moved. If the Region was opened from the Audio window, the bottom numerical changes to show the Anchor position. If the Region was opened from the Arrange window, the top numerical changes to show the start position, because the Anchor stays fixed in that case.

Moving the Anchor in the Audio window always shifts the Region while keeping the Anchor's Bar Ruler position in the Arrange window fixed. In the Sample Editor, you can turn that behaviour off using the Edit menu's Update Arrange Position option.

Regions and selections

Although the selection (dark area) initially matches the Region, you can move and resize the selection without affecting the Region:

- Click-drag to create a new selection.
- Shift-click-drag to extend the selection at either end.
- Use the Hand tool to drag the whole selection in either direction.

Once you've trimmed a perfect loop and made it a Region, use the Hand tool to create other Regions of the same size.

When you have a loop selected in the Sample Editor and you want to calculate its tempo, select a Tempo Alternative that you're not using, set the Locators to the length of the loop in bars, the select Adjust Tempo by Selection Length & Locators from the Sample Editor's Functions menu. That works when you open the Sample Editor from the Project Manager (see Chapter 12) as well – even when the audio file is not in the Audio window.

- Start playback from the Sample editor to hear the current selection. Use the Sample editor's Cycle button to continuously repeat the selection.

Once you've made a selection, you can either make it a new Region or use it to replace the original Region. If you've botched things up, you can recapture the original Region as the selection and start over.

M   Sample Editor » Edit » Selection -> Region
KC   Selection -> Region *«SH CO R»*
M   Sample Editor » Edit » Create New Region
KC   Create New Region *«CO R»*
M   Sample Editor » Edit » Region -> Selection
KC   Region -> Selection *«SH R»*

Playback from the Sample editor

The Sample editor has its own key commands for audio playback. As with the Audio window (see Chapter 9), keys assigned to those functions are freed for other uses when the Sample editor is not the top window. The Sample editor offers several Region-based options not found in the other windows.

KC   Play/Stop Selection *«Space»*
KC   Play/Stop All *«CT Space»* (All means the entire audio file)
KC   Play/Stop Region (which may be different than the selection)
KC   Play/Stop Region to Anchor *«SH OP Space»*
KC   Play/Stop Region from Anchor *«OP Space»*

Crossing zero

The Edit menus in the Arrange, Audio, and Sample editor windows have an option called Search Zero Crossings. The setting is independent for each window. When turned on, any changes to Region boundaries, the Anchor, or selection endpoints in the Sample editor will snap to the closest sample with value zero (the closest zero crossing). The purpose of that is to reduce the chance of clicks during sample playback, but it also may prevent you from exactly positioning and sizing a Region.

Typically the distance to the next zero crossing will be small enough to be musically imperceptible. The one exception is when you are looping a Region. In that case, the difference increases with each repetition of the loop, and the loop can get out of sync very quickly. The solution is to use copies (Shift-Option-drag) instead of looping the Region.

Destructive editing

Destructive editing refers to any process that physically changes the data in the audio file on your hard drive. Most of the operations on the Sample editor's Functions menu as well as most of the process on the Factory menu are destructive. Functions menu operations include: normalization and gain change, fade-in and –out, silence, invert and reverse, trim, and remove DC offset. (Time stretching Regions in the Arrange window is also a destructive process – see Chapter 3.)

More extensive audio processing, usually involving a dialog box with a variety of settings, are offered on the Factory (short for 'Digital Factory') menu:

- The Time Machine allows independent time and pitch shifting with formant correction.
- The Groove Machine adds swing by offsetting the audio at even 1/8th- or 1/16th-note positions while leaving the audio at odd positions unchanged. Needless to say, the results depend on the appropriateness of the original material. To use your own groove template, rather than being limited to 1/8th- or 1/16th-note swing, try the Factory's Quantize Engine.
- The Audio Energizer increases perceived level using a technique similar to mild tape saturation. It is intended for use after normalization to give the audio an additional bump.
- The Silencer both removes clicks and lowers the noise floor.

You can backup the audio file as well as revert to the backup from the Sample editor's Audio File menu. (The backup has the same name as the original followed by 'dup' and is saved in the same location.)

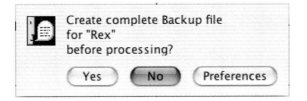

Figure 10.02
Before performing a destructive edit for the first time on an audio file, Logic gives you the opportunity to create a backup file just in case. The Preferences button opens the Audio Preferences, where you can turn this feature off. It also serves as a Cancel button in case you don't want to carry out the operation.

Time and Pitch Machine

The Time and Pitch Machine (TPM) is for time, pitch, and formant shifting selected parts of an Audio file. It uses the same algorithm as time shifting in the Arrange
window, which you can choose from the Algorithm menu at the bottom of the TPM
window (see Figure 10.03). You can use the graphic to set all three factors at once,
by click-dragging on the ball in the centre of the graphic. Fine adjustments are difficult to make that way, so a better choice is to use the numerical displays in the
right half of the window.

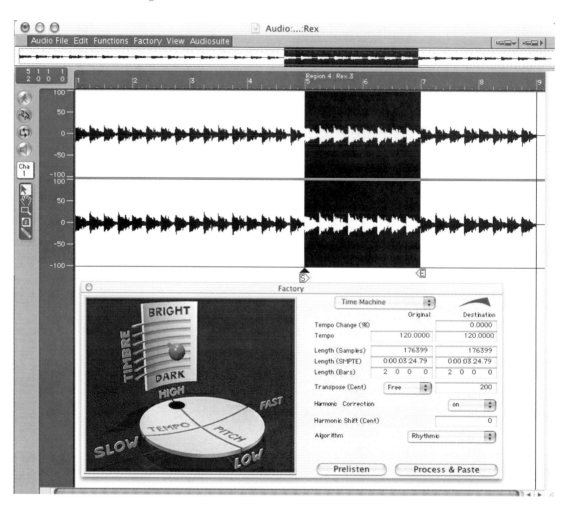

Figure 10.03

The Digital Factory's Time and Pitch
Machine allows you to perform three
operations: time stretching, pitch shifting,
and formant shifting. Those operations can
be performed separately or in combination.

The top five lines are used to control the time shift in any of five convenient
units: percent, tempo, samples, SMPTE, or Bars. The next line controls pitch shift
in cents – a semitone is 100 cents. Pitch shifting can be free or classic style as chosen from the menu to the left of the numerical. In classic mode, time and pitch are
shifted together, just as would happen if you were changing the speed of a tape
machine. But, unlike a tape machine, formant shift can still be controlled independently. The bottom two lines, labelled Harmonic Shift, turn formant shifting on
and set the amount.

Info

The Time shift section displays both the original and destination values. Only the destination values can be changed, except for the Tempo setting, which allows you to change the original as well. That's intended for cases in which the song tempo does not match the tempo of the audio file. In that case, if you know either the original tempo or the original bar length, you can change the original tempo to match — the bar display follows the tempo although you can't change it directly.

Quick tip

The intent of formant shifting is to compensate for pitch shifting – it allows you to change a baritone to a soprano rather than to a small child. (Well, that's wishful thinking, but you get the idea.) It can be an interesting effect in its own right, however. Try leaving the Transpose setting at zero and setting the Harmonic Shift to some non-zero value. Positive values represent smaller resonating bodies, while negative values represent larger ones.

Info

The Time and Pitch Machine's Prelisten button always uses a classic pitch shift regardless of the window's settings.

Swing and groove

In Chapter 7 we discussed using beat slicing and Rex files to change the groove and timing of an audio file. The Digital Factory's Groove Machine and Quantize Engine can often be used for that without slicing up the original file.

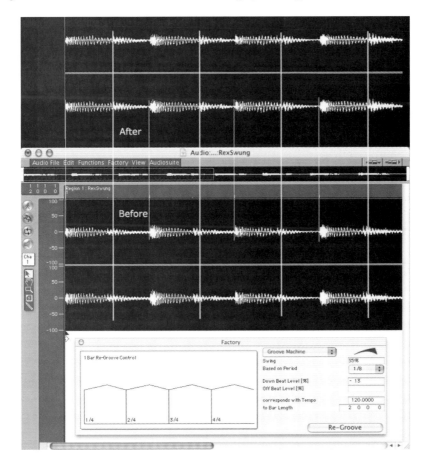

Figure 10.04
The Groove Machine can be used to add 8th- or 16th-note swing to an audio file. Here alternate 8th-notes have been moved 5% later (long vertical lines) while the others have been left unchanged (short vertical lines). At the same time the alternate 8th-note sections have been increased in level.

The Groove Machine simply offsets alternating 8th- or 16th-note sections of the audio file by a fixed percentage while leaving the others unchanged in time. It is useful for adding swing much as you would when using a swing quantize on a MIDI file.

The Quantize Engine attempts to apply grooves from Logic's quantize menu to audio files by selectively time stretching and shrinking segments of the file. It's a complex process that produces mixed results, and making a backup of the original audio file is strongly advised.

To use the Quantize Engine, first select the desired quantize groove from the Quantize By drop-down menu. Logic's default quantize grooves as well as any you've created in your song are available.

The three rows of short vertical lines represent from top to bottom: the 'hits' that Logic has found in the sound file, the grid of your quantize groove, and the resulting 'hits' that the Quantize Engine will realign the file to. You can click any of the lines in the top row to remove it from the quantize grid, thus correcting for false hits found by Logic. Adjusting the Granulation, Attack Range, Smooth Release, and

Figure 10.05
The Quantize Engine allows you to re-groove an audio file to match Logic's quantize templates or any you create. You can use it together with the Audio to Groove Template operation to match one audio file's groove to another's. Here the swing introduced by the Groove Machine in the previous example has been removed by the Quantize Engine.

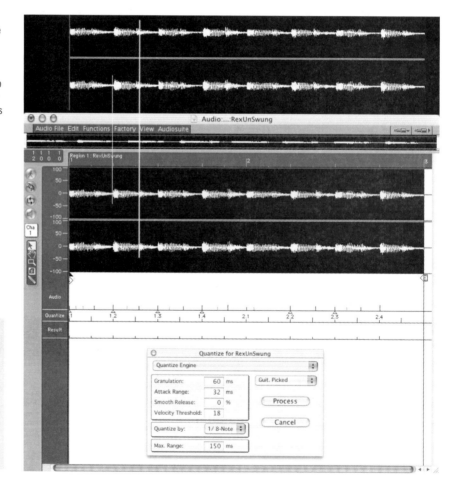

Quick tip

To match the groove of two audio files, try using Audio to MIDI Groove Template on the file whose groove you want to keep, then applying the Quantize Engine to the other audio file with the groove template just produced. As always, using one or two bars for a groove template produces the best results.

Velocity Threshold parameters will also refine the grid – but do that before deleting individual hit points, because any parameter change undoes your individual modifications.

The Audio to MIDI Groove Template operation has settings similar to the Quantize Engine's, but it generates a MIDI file to use as a groove template on other data rather than modifying your audio file. It requires some fiddling and experimentation like the Quantize Engine, but can produce a reliable groove from appropriate material.

Extracting Regions from audio CD tracks

In Chapter 7 we looked at Logic's Strip Silence function, which can be invoked from the Audio or Arrange window, for beat slicing. That is also an excellent way to extract individual loops and hits from audio sampling CDs that feature several examples on each CD track. Here are the steps:

- Add the CD track to the Audio window and invoke Strip Silence.
- Set a relatively high minimum time to accept as silence – 500 milliseconds or more usually works well.
- Strip Silence to produce Regions for each section of the track.
- Delete and resize Regions in the Audio window as needed to get rid of false selections and combine accidentally split ones (if any).
- Scroll through the Regions in a floating Audio window, editing the end points and Anchor of each Region in a linked Sample editor window as needed.

Splitting stereo files

There may be occasions when you want to split a stereo file into two mono files – one for each stereo channel. Here's how:

- Temporarily check the Audio Preference (in the Global box at the bottom) labelled 'Force record & convert interleaved into split stereo file(s)'
- If the target file is already in the Audio window, delete it. (Don't delete it from your hard drive, of course.)
- Add the target stereo audio file to the Audio window. Respond to the resulting dialog box by clicking the Convert button. You will now have two new files, labelled 'L' and 'R' representing the two channels of the original stereo file. The same files will have been created on your hard drive.
- Remove the file from the Audio window again, and rename the files on your hard drive without the 'L' and 'R' extensions. You can now load them as separate mono files.
- Don't forget to uncheck the Audio Preference to split stereo files, unless you want to continue working in that mode.

Quick tip

You can often use extreme EQ to heighten the groove in an audio file and get better results from Audio to MIDI Groove Template. First make a copy of the audio file, then place the Region from which you want to take the groove on an Audio Track. Insert a Channel EQ plug-in and use extreme boost and cut bands to bring out the hits you want in the groove—the kick or snare or hihat, for example. Bounce the EQ'd file and use it with Audio to MIDI Groove Template.

Quick tip

You can combine any pair of mono files into a stereo file by first renaming them with the same name followed by '.L' and '.R' suffixes. Then choose Convert to AIFF Stereo or Convert to Wave Stereo from the Audio window's Audio File menu. The original files will be unchanged and a new stereo file will be created.

Using plug-ins

Logic comes with a large variety of digital signal processing (DSP) plug-ins as well as supporting plug-ins in VST (Virtual Studio Technology) in OS 9 and Windows and AU (Audio Units) in OS X. Audio plug-ins can be either audio instruments (AIs), which respond to MIDI note messages, or audio effects, which do not. AIs can only be inserted into Audio Instrument objects, while audio effects can be inserted into almost any Audio object, including Audio Instrument objects. (See Chapter 4 for a detailed description of Audio objects.)

Inserting and controlling effects and instruments

Figure 11.01

Logic's seven types of Audio objects showing how plug-in effects and instruments are inserted. The two most used Audio objects are the Audio Track object (top track and left channel strip) and the Audio Instrument object (second track and second channel strip from left). The other objects in top down order are Aux and Bus objects for send-effect processing, the Rewire object of receiving input from Rewire slave applications, and Audio Input and Output objects for managing audio to and from your audio interface.

Audio effects are inserted into the signal path using the slots at the top of an Audio object. Initially there are two empty slots, but as soon as you fill both of them, a new slot appears. You can insert up to 15 effects per Audio object provided your CPU can handle it.

Audio instruments are inserted in the top slot of the section labelled 'I/O', and of course, they are only available in Audio Instrument objects. (That slot doesn't exist for some Audio objects and is used to select the input for other objects.)

Sends and returns

Most Audio objects have send slots for routing their output to Logic's 32 (optionally 64) send buses. You can have up to 16 sends per object. The Bus and Output objects are exceptions. The Bus object controls the return of the bus to the output and the Output object, being last in the signal path, has no need of sends.

Buses are typically used for effects that you want to apply to several signals simultaneously. Reverb and delay-related effects such as phasing, flange, and chorus often fall into this category.

Outputs

All Audio objects have an output selector except the Output object, whose output is fixed by its definition. For the others, the bottom menu in the I/O section is where you set the object's output. For outputs you can choose among the outputs of your audio interface, Logic's buses, or the Surround outputs. You can also select No Output, which is the typical choice when you're using Bus objects to feed multiple Aux objects, for example.

The plug-in window

Each audio effects or audio instrument plug-in has its own control panel that automatically opens in a floating window when the plug-in is inserted into an Audio object slot. You can reopen the window after closing it, by double-clicking on the plug-in name in the slot.

Info

All Audio objects always have the same number of insert slots, and you can insert effects into any of them – you don't need to start at the top, although that's the most logical approach. You can move effects around after they are inserted without losing their settings, by using the Audio Configuration window (see below).

Info

The Aux object can also function as a bus return, and it is more flexible because it has sends of its own, allowing you to form complex signal paths. If there is no Bus object, the Aux object gets its signal directly from the bus selected as its input. If there is a Bus object, it comes first, so that its volume, pan, and plug-ins all affect the Aux object's input.

Quick tip

You can only have one Bus object for any bus, but you can have many Aux objects feeding off of the same bus. You might use two Aux objects to construct your own independent right and left delay lines, for example. When several Aux objects have the same input, it's a good idea to also have a Bus object to control the overall feed level as well as to hold any plug-ins you want to use before the Aux plug-ins.

Figure 11.02
The Editor view of Logic's Platinumverb reverb plug-in. The controls along the top include the familiar Link button, the info button for exposing additional settings (not shown), the Bypass button, which also turns the effect off and saves CPU, the settings menu for loading and saving settings, two drop-down menus for selecting the Audio object and slot for display in the window, and the menu to toggle between Editor and Controls view.

Quick tip

If you hold the Command and Option keys while opening the plug-in window, it will open as a normal, non-floating window.

Info

Some Logic plug-ins have additional settings that don't show up on the Editor control panel. That is indicated by a Info button with a 0's and 1's icon, next to the Link button. Clicking it on will reveal sliders for the extra settings at the bottom of the plug-in window.

Quick tip

When auditioning a new plug-in, it is often convenient to step through the supplied presets. For Logic plug-ins, there are key commands for that purpose. For plug-ins from other manufacturers, you can usually use MIDI program change messages to select presets, and many MIDI hardware controllers have a built-in next/previous program feature that will send incremental MIDI program change messages. (If you're adventurous, you can also build a little Environment patch for that purpose.)

Quick tip

By default the plug-in window opens with its Link button turned off, which means that each effect will have its own window. You can avoid this proliferation of floating windows (which are always on top) by turning the Link button on (pink).

The plug-in controls may be viewed in two forms: Controls and Editor. The Editor view shows the graphic panel provided by the plug-in designer (if there is one). The Controls view is organized as columns of horizontal sliders with numerals on their left to show and type in values. The Editor view is usually more useful, but the Controls view can be handy when you're setting up Region Based Automation (see Chapter 6), because that's sometimes the only way to figure out which MIDI message controls which slider.

Plug-in settings

Logic has its own plug-in settings management scheme, which is accessed from the drop-down menu with the downward wedge icon. You can use it to load, save, copy, and paste settings. Plug-in settings are automatically saved in a folder named 'Plug-In Settings' in the same directory as the Logic application. When a plug-in is used for the first time, a folder within that folder with the plug-in's name is created and will automatically be used to hold all settings you create. You can further organize your plug-in settings using sub-folders within that folder.

Quick tip

If you have versions of Logic in more than one location, for example OS 9 and OS X versions, you can use an alias of the Plug-In Settings folder in one of those locations, thereby keeping all your plug-in settings in a single location.

Logic plug-ins use Logic's settings scheme exclusively, but other plug-ins typically have their own preset management scheme including loading and saving banks to disk. In case both exist, it's usually preferable to use the plug-in's own system because factory presets and presets from other users will usually be in that form.

Sidechains

Some plug-ins either require, or can optionally use two audio inputs. An example is a vocoder, which uses one input for the carrier (usually an instrument sound) and another for the program (usually spoken voice). Another example is a compressor, which can use a one input to control the compression and the other to be processed by it – an effect called ducking.

When an audio effects or audio instrument plug-in supports sidechain inputs, you will see a drop-down menu labelled 'Side Chain:' at the top of the plug-in window. From it you can select any Audio track, bus, or input from your audio interface.

Lookahead induced delay

Many of Logic's dynamics plug-ins have a lookahead feature, whereby the plug-in looks ahead in the audio file being processed to calculate its effect. Plug-ins that have this feature include: Limiter, Enveloper, Multipressor, Silver Gate, Noise Gate, and Ad-Limiter. All but Ad-Limiter have a lookahead control for setting the lookahead time in milliseconds. The maximum lookahead time depends on the plug-in and ranges from 10 ms for the Limiter to 100 ms for the Enveloper. The Ad-Limiter has a fixed lookahead time of roughly 100 ms. For all the others, the lookahead time can be set as low as zero (no lookahead).

Whenever lookahead is applied, a delay in processing equal to the lookahead time is induced. That applies during playback of audio files, during bouncing, and when playing audio instruments live or from MIDI Regions. There are several ways to compensate for this.

- In Logic's Audio Preferences there is an option called 'Plug-in delay compensation', which in effect jogs playback of the affected track (audio or audio instrument) to offset for the delay induced by the plug-in. That works for the Ad-Limiter as well as third party plug-ins that support it. It does not work for the Logic plug-ins that allow you to set the lookahead time.
- You can use the Region Delay Parameter to manually adjust playback earlier (negative delay setting) by the required amount. The delay adjustment is in ticks (1/960th of a beat), which at 120 BPM is approximately 0.5 milliseconds.
- You can actually move the Region back in time by the necessary amount to compensate for the lookahead delay.
- You can set the lookahead time to zero – lookahead is not necessary in many cases.

Quick tip

When you insert a plug-in with lookahead at the end of the signal path – in an Audio output object, for example – delay is not an issue, because everything is delayed. That applies when you use compression or limiting in a finalizing situation, for example.

The Audio Configuration window

M   Audio » Audio Configuration…
KC   Audio Configuration…

If you have a lot of audio tracks and instruments using many plug-ins,

Figure 11.03
The Audio Configuration window gives you a bird's eye view of all your plug-in slots. You can use it to insert plug-ins as well as to

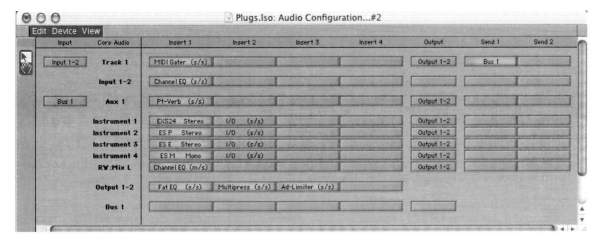

managing the plug-ins in the Environment or Mixer window can be tedious. Furthermore, you can't drag them around in either of those windows. The Audio Configuration window is designed for that.

The Audio Configuration window's View menu offers three views: All Components, Used Components, and I/O Labels. All Components view includes the full complement of inputs, outputs, instruments, auxes, and buses that your audio interface supports, subject to the choices you've made in the Audio Hardware & Drivers Preferences. The Used Components view includes only those you have created Audio objects for, and is obviously the more relevant view. The I/O Labels view allows you to create a custom label for each audio input, output, and bus.

The Audio Configuration window has two tools: Selector (arrow icon) and Hand. The Selector tool allows you to select inserts for any slot, just as you would on the Audio object's channel strip. The Hand tool allows you to click-drag plug-ins from slot to slot. If you hold the option key, a copy is made. When you move or copy a plug-in, its settings are copied with it.

Using Audio Instruments

Audio Instruments behave somewhat differently from external MIDI devices. They also respond differently to MIDI coming from an external MIDI keyboard than they do to MIDI coming from the playback of MIDI Regions in the Arrange window.

Multi-channel versus Multiple Output Instruments

Some audio instrument plug-ins are multi-channel, allowing you to play different sounds using different MIDI channels. Some audio instrument plug-ins allow you to route different voices to different audio outputs. In the latter case the output destination might be determined by the MIDI channel, the note pitch, the selected sample for sample players, or some other parameter.

Audio instrument plug-ins that support multiple MIDI channels usually have front panel buttons or menus for switching the front panel among the channels. That changes the program displayed on the control panel, but doesn't change what you're hearing when you play the instrument. The MIDI channel of the notes being played by the instrument controls which program you're hearing.

Audio instrument plug-ins that support multiple output channels appear in the Multi-Channel sub-menu of the Audio Instrument object's plug-in menu. Despite the name 'Multi Channel', plug-ins found there support multiple outputs, but may or may not be multi-channel in the above sense. Some audio instrument plug-ins have both stereo and multiple-output versions, in which case you will find them on both the Stereo and Multi Channel sub-menus.

Layering Audio Instruments

Logic gives processing priority to a single Audio Instrument object, keeping it in *Live* mode at all times. All other Audio Instrument objects are kept in *Sleep* mode. That has no impact on Region playback, because Logic wakes them up in time, but if you try to layer them for real-time playback, all but one will exhibit unacceptable latency. Logic's I/O plug-in in the Helpers section can be used to force an audio instrument to stay in Live mode.

The trick is to insert an I/O plug-in in the top audio effects slot for each audio

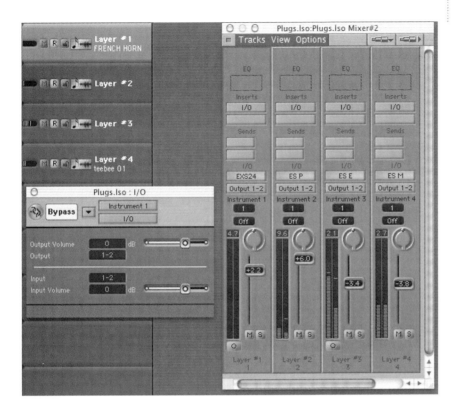

Figure 11.04
Logic's I/O plug-in, though not intended for
that purpose, will allow you to layer audio
instruments. You need to ensure that the I/O
plug-in's Output and Input settings are real
(i.e. not '——') and that the plug-in is in
Bypass mode.

instrument. The I/O plug-in has Output and Input settings that must be set to real ports for it to be effective. The purpose of the I/O plug-in is to route audio in and out of Logic for processing by external hardware devices. Since that intercepts the signal from the Audio Instrument object, you need to put the I/O plug-in in Bypass mode. It then keeps the audio instrument in Live mode without affecting the signal.

There are several ways you can get MIDI to multiple Audio Instrument objects at the same time. All of them require that Logic's transport be running:

- Click the Record button for each track assigned to an Audio Instrument object that you want to include in the layer.
- Create a neutral Environment object, such as a Monitor object, and cable it to each of the Audio Instrument objects you want to include in the layer. Then assign the Monitor object to an Arrange window track and select that track. Incoming MIDI will then be routed to all Audio Instrument objects in the layer.
- Use a non-neutral Environment object, such as a Channel Splitter, and cable a different output to each of the Audio Instrument objects you want to include in the layer. The MIDI channel of incoming notes will then determine which audio instrument plays. That's a good method if you have several players with separate keyboards, or are using a split keyboard controller that assigns each side of the split to a different MIDI channel.

Using Rewire slave instruments

Logic allows both MIDI and audio communication with Rewire aware applications such as Propellerhead Reason. Logic must be the master application and must be launched first. The other application must be the slave and must be launched second.

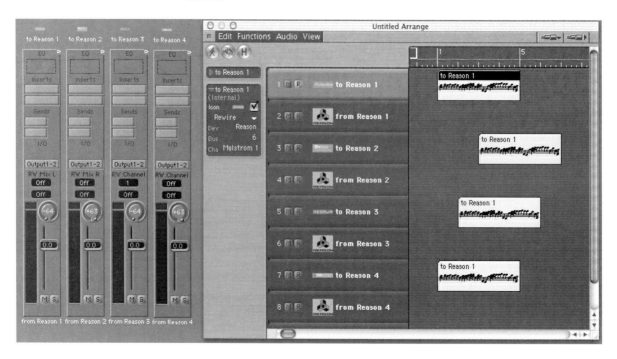

Figure 11.05
Logic uses special Environment objects called Rewire objects to send MIDI to Rewire 2 aware applications such as Propellerheads' Reason. Audio is returned from the Rewire application via Audio objects assigned to Rewire buses. You can use Logic's Bounce operation to capture the audio in audio files.

Quick tip

Logic has two modes of Rewire: Live and Playback. Live mode provides low latency operation but requires more CPU. Use Live mode when you're playing a Rewire instrument live. For MIDI Region playback, save the CPU and use Playback mode. The mode is set in the Audio Hardware & Drivers section of Logic's Preferences.

Quick tip

When you use Logic for live MIDI communication with a Rewire device, ensure the device's own MIDI input is disabled or you may get doubled notes.

Two Environment objects are needed for communication between Logic and the other application: a Rewire object is used to send MIDI to the other application and an Audio object assigned to a Rewire bus is used to receive audio back from the other application. Those Environment objects need to be assigned to Arrange window tracks. MIDI Regions are played on the Rewire object tracks and audio is mixed on the Audio object tracks.

Logic's Bounce operation allows you to capture the audio from the slave application and you can use Surround bouncing (see below) to capture separate channels in separate audio files. The audio files can then be used instead of launching the slave application. Send and insert effects plug-ins can, of course, be applied directly to the Rewire audio or after the fact, to bounced audio files.

Quick tip

Rewire audio buses are always mono. Therefore you need two Audio objects, panned hard left and right to capture a stereo Rewire signal. If you assign them to the same group for volume and muting purposes, you need only one Arrange track and Mixer channel to control them both.

The Rewire Environment objects have three drop-down menus to control the destination of their MIDI playback. The *Dev* menu allows you to select the Rewire slave device in case more than one is running. The *Bus* menu allows you to choose a Rewire bus for the target device. Its meaning varies with the chosen slave application. For Reason the first five buses correspond to Reason's MIDI Preferences settings. Starting with bus 6, each device in the Reason rack is available as a direct destination. The *Cha* menu is where you to select the MIDI channel for the selected bus. In the case of Reason, the names of the devices in the Reason rack appear on the Cha menu.

Bouncing tracks and instruments to separate audio files

By default, Logic's Bounce operation renders the output of a single Audio Output object to produce a single mono or stereo audio file. You can select one of the Surround Modes from the Surround Bounce drop-down menu to create separate, mono audio files for each Surround output.

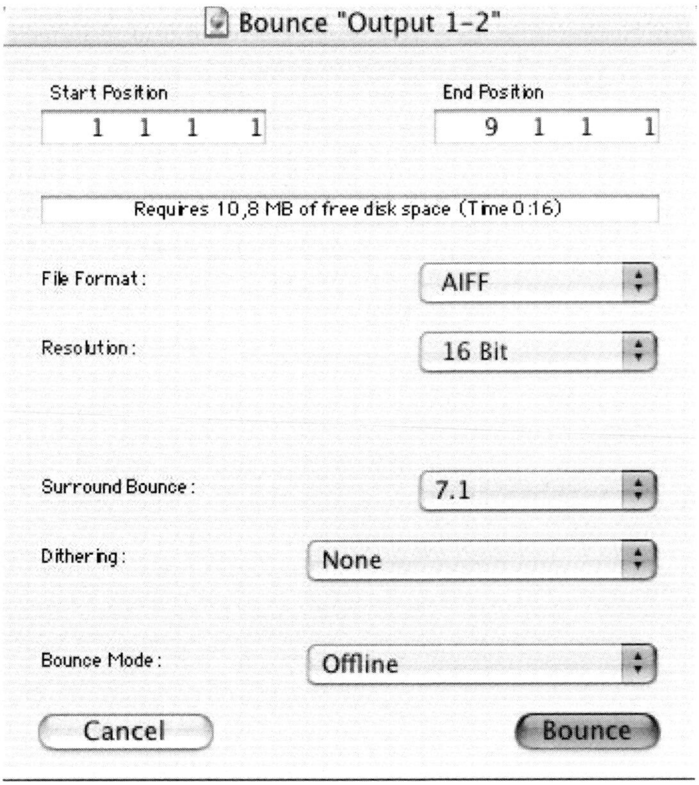

Figure 11.06
You can use the Surround Bounce menu in the Bounce dialog box to record bounce audio tracks and instruments to separate audio files. The Surround destinations are set up in the Surround Preferences dialog.

Info

Eleven different Surround setups can be defined in Logic's Surround Preferences. They range from three channel LCR to eight channel 7.1 setups. You can also control how the audio files are labelled in that window.

The Project Manager

T he Project Manager is Logic's window into your hard drive(s). It shows all file types relevant to Logic songs: song files, audio files, EXS24 instruments and their samples, Quicktime movies, and plug-in settings files. Those can be viewed by song or by category.

Figure 12.01
The Project Manager Tree display categorises the files in the Project Manager's database by type, sub-type (optional), and location. Selecting folders in the tree causes their contents to be displayed in the Project Manager's File window to the right of the tree (not shown).

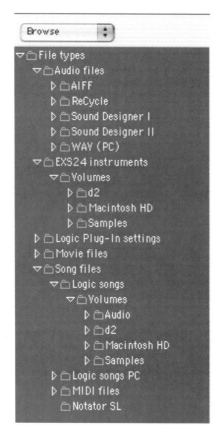

The Project Manager also includes tools for saving a song as a self-contained project (i.e. with all relevant files included), moving and copying files to other locations, and loading and editing audio files even when they are not included in a song.

Quick tip

Depending on your work preferences you can use the Project Manager to manage all audio files on all your hard drives or only files in selected locations. If most or all of your audio work is done in Logic, it's probably a good idea to use the Project Manager for everything, including importing audio files from new sampling CDs. If you use Logic as well as other audio software and many of your audio files are not used in Logic songs, you may prefer to be selective about what the Project Manager manages. Keeping the Project Manager completely up to date when you're creating audio files with other applications may not be worth the effort involved.

Creating the database

The first thing you must do to use the Project Manager is let it search some or all of your hard drives for files – a process called scanning. You can simply select Scan from its Functions menu and settle in for a long winter's nap, but a little prep work at the beginning can save you a bunch of time.

M   Project Manager » Functions » Scan
KC   Scan «CT S»
M   Project Manager » Functions » Abort Scan Process
KC   Abort Scan «CO .»

The drop-down menu at the top-left of the Project Manager window has four choices: Browse (the view you'll use most of the time), Find (a very powerful search engine that has numerous uses), Log (which is mainly for diagnostics), and Scan

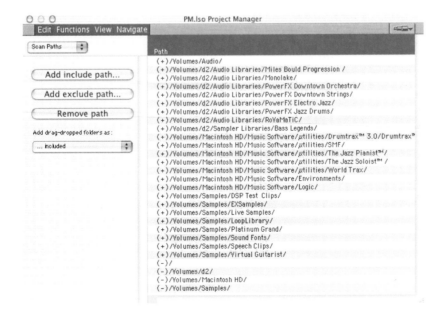

Figure 12.02
The Project Manager's Scan view is where you tell the Project Manager which directories to search and which to ignore in creating its database. The thing to remember is that you can include sub-paths of paths that have been excluded.

Paths (where you can tell the Project Manager where to look and not look for data).

The Scan view allows you to set up directory paths to be searched (called include paths) and to not be searched (called exclude paths). You can use the buttons in the left half of the window to add include and exclude paths, or you can simply drag drives and folders into the right half of the window from the Finder. In the latter case, the drop-down menu at the bottom controls whether the dragged-in paths are included or excluded.

The Project Manager also lets you scan individual folders. That's especially handy if you're not using the Project Manager for all your audio and song file management. When you create a song or use some audio files in a location the Project Manager doesn't have its database, simply scan the folder containing them.

M   Project Manager » Functions » Scan Folder
KC   Scan Folder *«CT D»*

Updating the Project Manager
Even if you let the Project Manager scan all your files, there's bound to come a time when its database loses touch with reality (meaning the true state of your hard drives). That can happen when:

- You rename a file in the Finder.
- You move or delete a file in the Finder.
- You work on a song in Logic without having the Project Manager database loaded.
- You create, move, or rename audio files with another application, which you also use in Logic songs.

When the Project Manager gets out of whack, you can usually fix things by:

- having the Project Manager check for modified or deleted files.

M   Project Manager » Functions » Check for modified or deleted files
KC   Check for modified or deleted files *«CT CO U»*

- having the Project Manager re-scan either specific folders or your entire system.

Where's the data?

The Project Manager keeps its database in hidden files – one for each hard drive. In OS X they are named 'LogicProject' and hidden in the root directory of each drive. In OS 9, they are named 'Logic PM Database' and again, hidden at the top level of each drive. The only way to remove a hard drive from the Project Manager's database is to delete the relevant hidden file. Hidden files can be found and deleted with various disk utilities including ResEdit and File Buddy from SkyTag software (www.skytag.com).

The Project Manager also maintains a reference file named 'Logic PMData', which is in the Preferences folder in either OS. To start over from scratch, delete that, too.

Using the Project Manager

Strictly speaking, using the Project Manager is optional – Logic is fully functional without it. But it can speed up your work as well as help with the organization of your hard drives and your Logic songs. Following are some useful applications for the Project Manager.

Consolidating Songs

Consolidating refers to the process of collecting all audio files and/or EXS24 instruments and their samples into a single project folder. The process can be invoked either from the Project Manager or Logic's Global File menu. Both methods produce the same results.

M   File » Save Song as Project…
M   Project Manager » Functions » Consolidate files of selected Songs…
KC Consolidate files of selected Songs… «CT CO C»

Figure 12.03
The Consolidate Song and Save Song as Project dialog box allows you to consolidate all files used by a song into a single project folder. You can choose for each file type, whether the files are moved, copied, or whether the song's references to them are left unchanged.

Consolidating a song involves some choices on your part that depend on the purpose of the consolidation. If you're archiving the song onto a CD ROM or back-up drive, you will probably want to copy all file types. Possible exceptions include Movies, which take lots of memory, and unused audio files, which you might prefer to remove from the song, but leave on your hard drive for future use. You might also not want to copy EXS instrument samples (or even the instruments themselves) if they are shared by other, unrelated songs and will be needed in this song only on the same computer (i.e. you're not taking the song to another location for further work).

If you're purpose in consolidating the song is to reorganize your hard drive, you will most likely want to move rather than copy some file types and leave others unchanged. Candidates for moving include used and unused audio files as well as EXS24 instruments and their samples that are used exclusively in versions of this song.

Whether you wish to include songs sharing files with the song you're consolidating usually depends on whether those songs are related. When unrelated songs share files, you will more likely want to copy those files or leave the song's references to them unchanged.

Whether you want the Project Manager to automatically delete empty folders after consolidating a song depends on whether those folders are used by other songs. For example, if you have a folder into which all Logic recording is done, you don't want to delete it just because a consolidation happens to empty it.

Auditioning and loading audio files

One of the Project Manager's best features is its ability to play and load audio files directly from its file window (the right half of the Project Manager window). When the file window is displaying a mix of file types, you can double-click an audio file to display only audio files in the same location. When the file window is displaying only audio files, each file has an Info wedge to its left. Clicking the wedge will

Figure 12.04
When the Project Manager's file window displays only audio files, you can view their waveform by clicking the Info wedge at their left. When the waveform is visible, you can audition it and open it in the Sample Editor just as you can from the Audio window.

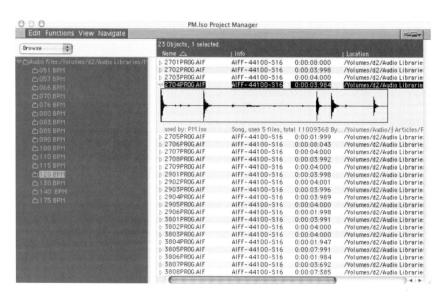

expose the audio file waveform, and as in the Audio window, you can click any-where in the waveform to play from that point to the end. The audio channel select-ed in the Audio window is used for playback.

Double-clicking on the waveform display will open the audio file in Logic's Sample Editor window. You can make changes, but the Project Manager will warn you if the file is used in any songs. You can also add selected audio files to the cur-rent song and optionally place them in the Arrange window at the SPL position. You will be given the option of using existing track(s) or creating new ones.

Quick tip

You can sort the list of files in the Project Manager's file window by clicking any of the column labels at the top. The current sort-column is indicated by a wedge, which you can click to reverse the sort order.

Quick tip

Auditioning and adding audio files using the Project Manger is much more convenient than using the Audio window or the Finder, because it gives you access to all scanned files regardless of their location. Used in conjunction with the Project Manager's Find function (see below), you can save tons of time poking around through folders trying to find specific files.

Finding stuff

The Project Manager's Find feature is another big timesaver. It allows you to select files of each type using various criteria and then displays the results in the file window. You can select and operate on those results just as in the Browser view.

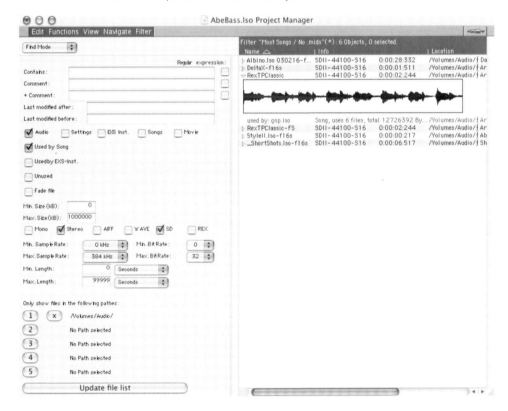

Figure 12.05

The Project Manager's Find view allows you to search its database for specific file types meeting specific conditions. The found files are displayed in the file window and can be manipulated just as in the Browser view. Here all stereo audio files in Sound Designer II format on the volume named 'Audio' that are used in songs are found. The file view shows the waveform and info for one of the found files.

Quick tip

The Project Manager lumps MIDI files with Logic song files. There's no way to search for just Logic songs, but if you set a minimum size of around 100 KB, most songs will be included and most MIDI files won't.

Quick tip

The used and unused criteria in the Project Manager's Find window apply to all songs in the Project Manager's database. Files used by individual songs, can of course, be found by clicking the info wedge next to the song listing in the file window.

Here are some things you can do with it:

- Find all songs with unresolved cross references to other file types. Once found, you can select some or all of them and use the Project Manager's Find unresolved file references for selected items function to attempt to fix them.

M   Project Manager » Functions » Find unresolved file references for selected items
KC   Find unresolved file references for selected items *«CT U»*

- Find all EXS24 instruments used/unused in any song in the Project Manager database. From the resulting list, you can click the info triangles next to the listed items to view what song each instrument is used in as well as what samples are used in the instrument.
- Find all files whose name or Project Manager comment fields contain specified text. If you regularly use comments or filename extensions of a particular format, you can find them all this way.

Quick tip

Comments are an excellent way to categorise and locate files. The Project Manager allows two comments per file (of any type) and furthermore, allows you to set them for multiple files at once.

- Find all files in up to five selected paths that match any criteria.

Quick tip

The five buttons at the bottom of the Find view window allow you to specify which directories are searched. When none are used, the entire Project Manager database is searched.

Appendix 1
Troubleshooting

H ere are ways to approach some of the more common problems you might encounter, especially when you're setting up Logic for the first time.

No MIDI input

If the right things aren't happening when you play notes on your MIDI keyboard here are some things to check:

• Look at the at the MIDI Activity Display at the top-right of the Transport window. When nothing is happening it should display 'No In' on top and 'No Out' on the bottom. When you play a single note, the No In display should change to show a note symbol, MIDI channel, note pitch, and velocity.
• If the MIDI Activity Display shows incoming MIDI notes, then they are getting to the selected track in the Arrange window. If they're not playing the plug-in or external MIDI device you expect the problem is either with the plug-in settings, the MIDI device, or the setup of the Environment object assigned to that track. For help with the latter problem, see Chapter 4.
• If the MIDI Activity Display does not show incoming MIDI notes, the first place to look is the Clicks & Ports Layer of the Environment. If there is a Physical Input object, try deleting it. If there is still no MIDI Activity Display, the problem is either with your MIDI controller, your MIDI interface, the MIDI setup in your operating system, or Logic's Communication Preferences (OS 9 only).
• If deleting the Physical Input object solves the problem, then there is a problem with how it was cabled. If you have Environment processing between the Physical Input and the to Sequencer object, the problem is probably there.

No MIDI output

If you have MIDI input, and have selected an Arrange window track assigned to an Environment object set up for an external MIDI device, but that device is not playing here are some things to check:

• Look at the MIDI Activity Display at the top-right of the Transport window. When nothing is happening it should display 'No In' on top and 'No Out' on the bottom. When notes are being played either from a MIDI Region or live, the No Out display should change to show the notes being sent out.

- If the MIDI Activity Display is not showing notes being sent out, the problem is probably with the setup of the Environment object assigned to the selected track. See Chapter 4 for help in setting up MIDI Instrument objects in the Environment.
- If the MIDI Activity Display is showing notes being sent out, the problem is probably with your external MIDI device setup, your MIDI interface, or the MIDI setup in your operating system. If they have LEDs to indicate MIDI activity, check to see if they are flashing. If not, the problem is probably with the operating system setup. (Your MIDI interface and receiving MIDI device are turned on, right?)

External MIDI device Is playing double notes

If your MIDI keyboard is part of a MIDI receiving device and playing notes on the keyboard causes double notes, the device probably has Local Control turned on. Disconnect the device's MIDI input from Logic and see if playing the keyboard causes notes to sound. If so, that's the problem – the device is receiving notes both directly from the keyboard and from Logic.

Most modern MIDI devices that include keyboards have an option to turn Local Control off. Consult your manual. If you can't turn Local Control off, you have two options. On the MIDI Options page of Logic's Song Settings, there's a setting called 'Instrument without MIDI Thru function', which by default is set to Logic's No Output object. Click the words 'No Output' and select the Environment Instrument object you use for that MIDI device.

Alternatively, you can create an Environment Fader object, cable it into the Instrument for the offending device, assign it to the Arrange track instead of the Instrument, and set the Fader's Filter parameter to 'Thru' in the Parameter Box.

Playing MIDI results in a MIDI feedback loop

This is similar to the double notes problem, but results from the MIDI Thru setting on your MIDI device. MIDI Thru should be turned off. Otherwise, when you play a note, it passes through Logic and back to the MIDI device, which passes it back to Logic, which passes it back to the MIDI device, etc. If you can't turn MIDI thru off, you can use the same tricks as for double notes, but that may require you to find and turn Local Control on – otherwise the keyboard won't play the MIDI device at all.

Hung MIDI notes

Hung MIDI notes can happen for many reasons: accidentally changing Arrange tracks while holding notes, using an Environment process that blocks, changes, or re-routes note-off messages, or some temporary glitch in your MIDI system, resulting from too much MIDI data, for example. If the problem is persistent, you need to track it down. If it is only occasional, click the MIDI Activity Display to send an All Notes Off message to your MIDI devices. If that doesn't work, double-click the display to send a separate note-off message for every possible note on every possible MIDI channel.

No MIDI to Rewire devices

If you're slaving another Rewire application such as Propellerhead's Reason to Logic, but it isn't receiving MIDI:

- Ensure that you have created Rewire objects in the Environment and routed them correctly for the Rewire slave application. See Chapters 4 and 10 for details.
- Ensure that you launch Logic first and the other Rewire application second.
- Ensure that the MIDI setup for the Rewire device is correct.

No audio from Rewire devices

If you're slaving another Rewire application such as Propellerhead's Reason to Logic, but the audio is not playing back in Logic, the problem is probably in the setup of the Audio objects in the Environment intended to receive the audio. In particular, you may have them set to the wrong Rewire buses (see Chapters 4 and 10). Try other bus settings – trial and error is the only solution. Also make sure the other Rewire application has its outputs set to Rewire buses.

Audio Instrument plug-in latency

If this occasionally happens, the problem is that Logic has not put the Audio Instrument in Live mode for some reason. Select a different track, then re-select the track for the Audio Instrument. Also try starting Logic playing.

If this is a permanent problem for all Audio Instruments, it probably has to do with the I/O Buffer Size setting in Logic's Audio Driver Preferences. Large buffer sizes result in high latency – lower settings use more CPU. You should be able to find a suitable compromise that produces low latency. If the I/O Buffer Size setting is not the problem, the problem is most likely with your audio interface or its drivers.

Can't synchronize audio to MIDI errors

When Logic throws up this error, it almost always means you're trying to play too many tracks using too many effects or audio instruments. Try freezing or muting some tracks.

One way to keep track of how your CPU is handling the load is to open the System Performance meter from the Audio menu. That shows both CPU and disk-access usage.

No audio input

If you're not getting any audio input, here are some things to check.

- If you're using an Audio Input object, check its meters to see if they are showing audio input. If not, the problem is with your setup, your audio interface, or Logic's Audio Drivers Preferences settings.

- If you're not using an Audio Input object, check the meters for the Audio track on which you're trying to record, and ensure its record switch is on.
- If the meters are showing audio input, but you're not hearing it, check the Audio Drivers Preferences to make sure Software Monitoring is turned on. That is required for any monitoring.
- Keep in mind that if the Audio Input object is set to an audio output, you will only hear it when no track for the same audio input is record-enabled. When a track is record-enabled, its output controls whether and how audio is heard. (Any processing by a plug-in in the Audio Input object will be heard in either case.)

Appendix 2
Key commands

T he following tables show key commands with default assignments. They are separated by window, just as in Logic's Key Command window.

Global commands

			*	Record
				• Record Repeat
				• Record Toggle
				• Capture Last Take as Recording
				• Capture Last Take as Recording & Play
			Enter	Play
			.	Pause
			0	Stop
			Space	Play or Stop
			[	Rewind
			]	Forward
			=	Set rounded Locators by Objects
			\	Swap Left and Right Locator
SH			Enter	• Play from Selection
SH			Space	• Goto Selection
	OP	CO	F1	Goto Marker Number 1
	OP	CO	F2	Goto Marker Number 2
	OP	CO	F3	Goto Marker Number 3
	OP	CO	F4	Goto Marker Number 4
	OP	CO	F5	Goto Marker Number 5
	OP	CO	F6	Goto Marker Number 6
	OP	CO	F7	Goto Marker Number 7
	OP	CO	F8	Goto Marker Number 8
	OP	CO	F9	Goto Marker Number 9
	OP	CO	F10	Goto Marker Number 10
	OP	CO	F11	Goto Marker Number 11
	OP	CO	F12	Goto Marker Number 12
	OP	CO	F13	Goto Marker Number 13
	OP	CO	F14	Goto Marker Number 14
	OP	CO	F15	Goto Marker Number 15
			/	Cycle
			S	Solo
	OP		S	• Set Solo Lock Mode
			C	MIDI/Monitor Metronome Click
SH			L	Lock/Unlock Current Screenset
			R	Copy MIDI Events...

		X	Extended Sequence Parameters...
OP		R	Recording options...
OP		M	MIDI options...
OP		P	Preferences...
	CO	I	Import File...
	CO	1	Open Arrange Window...
	CO	2	Open Track Mixer...
	CO	3	Open Score Editor...
	CO	4	Open Transform
	CO	5	Open Hyper Editor...
	CO	6	Open Matrix Editor...
	CO	7	Open Transport...
	CO	8	Open Environment...
	CO	9	Open Audio Window...
	CO	0	Signature/Key Change List Editor...
OP		E	Toggle Event Float
		E	Toggle Event Editor
		W	Toggle Sample Editor
OP		Y	Open System Performance...
OP		X	Open Synchronisation Window...
OP		T	Open Tempo List...
OP		K	Open Key Commands...
OP		C	Open Object Colors...
	CO	M	Open Movie...
		A	Set Audio Record Path ...
OP		W	Close Floating Window
	CO	W	Close Window or Song
SH		W	Select Next Window
	CO	N	New
	CO	O	Open...
OP	CO	W	Close
	CO	S	Save
OP	CO	S	Save Song as...
	CO	P	Print
	CO	Q	Quit
	CO	Z	Undo
SH	CO	Z	Redo
OP		Z	Undo History...
	CO	X	Cut
	CO	C	Copy
	CO	V	Paste
	CO	A	Select All

Various windows

		Esc	• Show Tools
	CT	Left	Zoom Horizontal Out
	CT	Right	Zoom Horizontal In
	CT	Up	Zoom Vertical Out
	CT	Down	Zoom Vertical In
		Z	Zoom to fit Selection vertically & horizontally, Navigation Snapshot
			Zoom to fit Selection horizontally, store Navigation Snapshot
			Zoom to fit Locators, store Navigation Snapshot
			Store Navigation Snapshot
SH		Z	Navigation: Back
		PageUp	Page Up
		PageDown	Page Down

			Top	Page Left
			Bottom	Page Right
			P	Hide/Show Parameters
		CT	G	Grid
			V	Catch Clock Position
			O	MIDI Out Toggle
			I	MIDI In Toggle
			M	Mute Objects

Arrange and various sequence editors

SH	CO		A	Deselect All
SH			T	Toggle Selection
SH			F	Select All Following
SH			I	Select inside Locators
SH			U	Select empty Objects
SH			O	Select overlapped Objects
SH			E	Select Equal Objects
SH			S	Select Similar Objects
SH			H	Select Equal Channels
SH			P	Select Equal Subpositions
SH			M	Select Muted Objects
			Left	• Select Previous Event
			Right	• Select Next Event
SH			Left	• Toggle Previous Event
SH			Right	• Toggle Next Event
SH			V	Scroll To Selection
			Tab	Note Overlap Correction
SH			Tab	Note Force Legato
SH			Up	Select Top Line
SH			Down	Select Bottom Line
			J	Merge Objects/Digital Mixdown
	CO		Y	Split Objects by Locators
			Y	Split Objects by rounded Song Position
		CT	Y	Split Objects by Song Position
		CT	P	• Pickup Clock (Move Event to SPL Position)
OP			Right	• Nudge Event Position by + Nudge Value
OP			Left	• Nudge Event Position by - Nudge Value
OP		CT	T	• Set Nudge Value to Tick
OP		CT	F	• Set Nudge Value to Format
OP		CT	B	• Set Nudge Value to Beat
				• Set Nudge Value to Bar
OP		CT	S	• Set Nudge Value to SMPTE Frame
OP			Up	• Event Transpose +1
OP			Down	• Event Transpose -1
			U	Positions/Time Ruler in SMPTE units

Arrange window

			Up	• Select previous Track
			Down	• Select next Track
			Left	• Select previous Object
			Right	• Select next Object
SH			C	Select Equal Colored Objects
	CO		F	Pack Folder
SH	CO		F	Unpack Folder
SH			Return	Create Track

SH		CT	Return	Create Track with next Instrument
		CT	H	Hide track
	OP	CT	H	Unhide all tracks
		CT	M	Mute Track
		CT	*	Record Enable Track
	CO		R	Find Original of Alias
SH			A	Select All Aliases of Object
	OP		J	Audio Crossfade Options for Merge...
SH			J	Merge Objects per Tracks
	CO		D	Demix by Event Channel
			T	Adjust Tempo using object length and Locators
		CT	R	Convert Regions to Individual Regions
		CT	F	Convert Regions to Individual Audio Files
		CT	S	Strip Silence
			N	Normalize
			Q	Fix Quantize
			L	Toggle Loop
			K	Turn Loops to Real Copies
			D	Erase Duplicated Events
			B	Set Optimal Object Sizes rounded by bar
		CT	B	Set Optimal Object Sizes rounded by denominator
		CT	Tab	Remove Overlaps
	OP	CT	Tab	Tie Objects by Length Change
SH		CT	Tab	Tie Objects by Position Change
	CO		J	Tie Sequences within Locators
		CT	E	Erase outside Object Borders
		CT	D	Delay in ms
		CT	O	Object Content
SH	OP		C	Instrument Colors To Objects
SH	OP		N	Tracknames To Objects

Environment window

		CT	Backspace	Clear Cables only
SH		CT	Left	Object move left
SH		CT	Right	Object move right
SH		CT	Up	Object move up
SH		CT	Down	Object move down
	OP	CT	Left	Object Width -1 Pixel
	OP	CT	Right	Object Width +1 Pixel
	OP	CT	Up	Object Height -1 Pixel
	OP	CT	Down	Object Height +1 Pixel
		CT	C	Hide/Show Cables
		CT	P	Protect Cabling/Positions
SH			T	Toggle Selection
SH			D	Select Cable Destination
SH			O	Select Cable Origin
			Tab	goto previous Layer
		CT	S	Cable serially

Score window

		CT	P	Explode Polyphony
	OP	CO	V	Paste Multiple
			Right	• Next Event
			Left	• Previous Event
			Down	• Next Staff

			Up	•Previous Staff
	CT		S	Stems: default
	CT		Top	Stems: up
	CT		Bottom	Stems: down
	CT		Backspace	Stems: hide
	CT		T	Ties: default
	CT		PageUp	Ties: up
	CT		PageDown	Ties: down
	CT		B	Beam Selected Notes
	CT		U	Unbeam Selected Notes
	CT		D	Default Beams
	CT		A	Default Accidentals
SH			#	Enharmonic Shift: #
SH			B	Enharmonic Shift: b
OP	CO		A	•Align Object Positions Vertically
	CO	CT	S	Open Score Style Window
	CO	CT	I	Open Instrument Set Window
	CO	CT	F	Settings: Global Format
	CO	CT	P	Score Preferences
SH		CT	Top	Insert: Slur Up
SH		CT	Bottom	Insert: Slur Down
SH		CT	C	Insert: Crescendo
SH		CT	D	Insert: Decrescendo

Event window

	Up	Scroll to Previous Event
	Down	Scroll to Next Event
CT	V	•Copy value to all following events

Hyper edit

CT	Return	Create Event Definition
CT	Backspace	Delete Event Definition
CT	T	Convert Event Definition...
CT	C	Copy Event Definition
CT	V	Paste Event Definition
CT	A	Auto define toggle

Audio window

	Up	Select Previous Audio File
	Down	Select Next Audio File
	Space	Play/Stop Region
CT	F	Add Audio File...
CT	R	Add Region
CT	Backspace	Delete File(s)
CT	O	Optimize File(s)
CT	B	Backup File(s)
CT	C	Copy/Convert File(s)
CT	M	Move File(s)
SH	U	Select Unused
CT	S	Strip Silence
CT	I	Import SDII Regions
CT	E	Export SDII Regions

Sample edit window

		Space	Play/Stop Selection
	CO	B	Create Backup
SH	CO	B	Revert to Backup
		Save A Copy As...	
SH	CO	S	Save Selection As...
SH		R	Region -> Selection
SH	CO	R	Selection -> Region
		Left	• Goto Selection Start
		Right	• Goto Selection End
		Down	• Goto Region Anchor
	CO	R	Create New Region
	CT	N	Normalize
SH	CT	G	Change Gain...
	CT	I	Fade In
	CT	O	Fade Out
	CT	Backspace	Silence
	CT	R	Reverse
		T	Trim
	CT	T	Time and Pitch Machine...
	CT	G	Groove Machine...
	CT	E	Audio Energizer...
	CT	M	Audio to MIDI Groove Template...

EXS24 Instrument editor

SH		T	Toggle Selection
		Up	Previous Zone/Group
		Down	Next Zone/Group
	CT	F	Open file selector for selected zone
	CT	Z	New Zone
	CT	G	New Group

Appendix 3
Places to go, things to read

ogic has a very active user community and there are a number of independent sources of publications about Logic. Here are some useful references.

Places to go on the Web

www.emagic.de
Emagic's Web site is the place for updates, news, and numerous useful links.

www.swiftkick.com
Visit my Web site for links, downloadable Environment patches including the Logic Users' Group Collection, and information on my Environment Toolkit.

www.omega-art.com
Hendrik Veenstra maintains an active site with articles, Environment downloads, and a compendious collection of frequently asked questions (and some answers, too).

groups.yahoo.com/group/logic-users
With over 10,000 members, the Logic Users Group is the most active of the lists devoted to Logic. Post a question there and it will undoubtedly be answered. You'll also find links to more specialized Logic lists there.

www.gearvision.com
Gear Vision produces and markets training videos for Logic by longtime guru and demonstration artist, Phil Jackson.

www.powerkeys.com
Powerkeys produces and markets a professionally tested key command set with computer keyboard overlays.

Things to read

Making Music with Emagic Logic Audio
by Stephen Bennett
PC Publishing — www.pc-publishing.com

Get Creative with Emagic Logic
by Keith Gemmell
PC Publishing — www.pc-publishing.com

Emagic Logic Virtual Instruments
by Stephen Bennett
PC Publishing — www.pc-publishing.com

The Logic Notation Guide
by Johannes Prischl
members.aon.at/prischl/LNG

Logic Power!
by Orren Merton
www.muskalipman.com

Index